Concepts & Illusions

Concepts & Illusions
A Perspective

Sabina Oberoi

RADHA SOAMI SATSANG BEAS

Published by:
J. C. Sethi, Secretary
Radha Soami Satsang Beas
Dera Baba Jaimal Singh
Punjab 143 204, India

First edition 2016

21 20 19 18 17 16   8 7 6 5 4 3 2

ISBN 978-81-8466-486-7

Printed in India by: Replika Press Pvt. Ltd.

TABLE OF CONTENTS

AUTHOR'S PREFACE

Think and then believe –
Believe and then speak –

We have the remarkable ability to create convenient conceptions and twist them into innovative interpretations. We weave wonderful webs of fantasies and fallacies, romanticize the path, misunderstand the teachings, squeeze pointless meanings from the Master's words, find excuses to escape from our commitments, and play the blame-game with the karma theory. Thus we totally digress from the reality, and move further and further away from the Master's teachings.

We complicate the simplicity of the teachings with our fancy illusions, concepts, and misinterpretations, instead of applying our common sense. The path is simple; we make it complicated!

The Enigma of a Master

Is the Master God?

Is he or isn't he? The most crucial and only test of our belief that the Master is God is, do we obey his wish for us to meditate? If we do not follow the one and only command *(hukam)* from the one we believe is the Master, then we are mocking our belief, we are pretentious about our belief – for who would have the gall to disobey the Master's commandment?

When we say the Master is God, is fear guiding our belief because we think our lives will go awry, and that eventually we will go to hell if we don't conform to the belief that Master is God? Do we convince ourselves of this theory to hide our doubts? Is it based on others' experience or our own personal experience? Is the theory inherited, handed down from family members? Do we claim that theory to avoid being branded as unbelievers?

Logically, we would ask, how can a human being be God? It sounds so absurd, it couldn't ever be possible. The idea naturally does not appeal to our intelligence, for how can someone who is an ordinary householder with parents, siblings, spouse, children and friends – who is born like us, eats, sleeps, walks and breathes like us, is vulnerable to bodily ailments, lives through old age and faces eventual death – how can that person be the invincible God?

We will have doubts and questions. When we don't have proof, how can we believe? Books cannot reveal the truth, because knowledge is not experience, nor can we learn from others' experience. Experience cannot be expressed; it can only be felt within oneself. On a spiritual path we walk alone. That's why we use the phrase *self*-realization; it can only be based on our own personal experience. And most of us don't have that!

Besides, we look for proof in everything – we question the creator and the creation – so how can we believe or claim the Master is God without substantial experience? It's a preposterous suggestion, a bizarre idea. We certainly hope he is – but we need to experience it to believe it. We also desperately want him to be, or we are in deep trouble.

Then again, if he is God, it means that God can also be a human being. But the idea that God could be human is confusing; it nullifies his mystery. This suggestion seems absolutely wacky! God is supposed to be all-pervading, all-encompassing, omnipresent – a superpower. If he is human, then he certainly is not God as we suppose him to be.

No! This theory is totally off the wall! Not acceptable. The Master is not God and neither is he human.

So if the Master is not God and God is not human, then what about another theory – that human beings are potential gods, that they possess the ability to achieve higher levels of spiritual consciousness, to achieve God-consciousness?

Just think! We could look at this argument with some semblance of optimism – there seems to be some degree of reason in this theory. Yes, we could all be potential gods. If "we are made in his image," as declared in the Bible, then this is a sure-shot possibility.

So for now, based on the above assumptions, let's go with the theory that the Master is not God, God is not human, and we mortals are all potential gods.

But first, to reveal the truth about the Master and our potentiality, we need to know who and where God is. Then we will take a reality check on the Master.

God Is Here, There, and Everywhere

Each one of us is born with an innate need to search for the truth. We don't learn how to do this, we don't cultivate or adopt this curiosity; it's an inherent part of our analytical, questioning mind. Our natural questions arise – "Who is the creator?" "Why did he make this universe?" "Who am I?" "Why am I here?" and so forth.

Well, we can break our heads against the wall for answers; but we will get broken heads and no answers. We can try intellectual analysis; we will still come to a dead end, because there are no answers. Even the greatest philosopher cannot answer questions about the creation. There could be some semblance of an understanding, but certainly no tangible, positive answers. No one who has ever walked this earth has been able to find a reasonable, logical answer to explain the creation and its mysteries. So we can keep asking why this, why that, and why the other, but there will still be no answer.

It's human nature to doubt the positive and believe in the negative because our mind naturally tilts towards negativity. That is the sheer nature of the mind. How many of us doubt that the devil exists? We seem to be amply convinced of the devil's existence without proof – we seem to be comfortable with the idea of the devil. We talk about it with a certain belief and conviction. We don't search for proof or question the existence of the devil, or Kal, because it is universally accepted.

But do we talk of God's existence with the same belief, the same confidence, the same conviction? Perhaps not. We are constantly looking for, asking, or reading about proofs of his existence. We shake from very roots and question the existence of God in times of adversity or calamity. Whether the existence of both God and the devil is known or unknown is debatable – yet, the theory of the devil's presence seems more credible because the mind is easily manoeuvred towards negativity. Yet we doubt the positive – that God exists.

A story is told about Sri Aurobindo. He was asked by a philosopher, "Do you believe in God?"

"No" he replied, "I do not believe in God."

The philosopher was shocked. "I thought you had seen God," he said.

Sri Aurobindo laughed. "Yes, I have seen God, that's why I say I don't believe. Belief is out of ignorance. I know. I don't believe."[1]

The world over, people believe in God without any proof that he exists. Science and technology, no matter how progressive, cannot prove his existence. They can give logical explanations for inventions and discoveries, as that which is limited can be based on logic. But God's creation is beyond the parameters of logic and reason – because it is unlimited, infinite, and therefore beyond our understanding. If we could understand God with our little minds, we wouldn't need him; but because the human mind is always doubting, questioning, and never satisfied, we would still be searching – for something.

Yet despite lack of any proof of God's existence, we live with a mysterious, ineffable feeling of his presence. Some part of us accepts him and even takes him for granted! In times of trouble, tragedy, crisis and disaster, we spontaneously clasp our hands in supplication and look up at the sky. In spite of our doubting minds, we have confidence that the sun will shine every morning and that the time of sunrise and sunset, of low tide and high tide, can be predicted. We have a fear of the unknown and yet we compensate for that fear with a belief in the ultimate unknown. This belief arises from a feeling deep within that tells us that a superpower does exist; we just don't understand it, cannot explain or express it. Just as a child cannot understand Einstein's theories, so too, our eyes cannot see beyond the horizon because our knowledge and understanding are limited.

Deep within our being, we cannot deny his existence. We feel him in nature all around us: in the depths of the sea, the majestic mountains, the magical snowflakes, the powerful sun, the soft moon, the joyful rain, the soothing flowers, the beautiful birds and animals. And yet, here is the duality – we also feel his presence in roaring thunder, crackling lightning, destructive floods, devastating famines, and life-shattering earthquakes and volcanoes.

We cannot deny his existence in the face of such power and mystery. Surely there is an overarching force at work, yet we are unable to penetrate the depths of that mystery.

God is here, there, and everywhere! That is his mystery. Every cell in our body knows that he is real, in all his might, despite his invisibility. There is no running away from it. We cannot use our intellect to unravel his elusiveness. He is too subtle, yet too vast to comprehend. He will always remain a mystery and a paradox.

The power of his existence lies in his concealment, and the mystery of his existence lies deep within us.

Deep Within Us

The Bible says: "Know ye not that ye are the temple of God, and that the spirit of God dwelleth in you?"[2]

According to Buddhism: "If you think the Law is outside yourself, you are embracing not the absolute Law but some inferior teaching."[3]

In Hinduism it is said: "He is the one God hidden in all beings...dwelling in all beings...."[4]

And in the Granth Sahib it is written: "Everything is within the home, nothing is outside. He who seeks outside is lost in illusion." *(sabh kichh ghar mah baahar naahi. baahar tolai so bharam bhulaahi.)*[5]

If so many scriptures preach the same theory, there must be some semblance of truth to it, even if we are doubtful. In which case it stands to reason that if God were to be discovered or revealed, the only way would be to reach him from within us, as he is "hidden in all beings."

All scriptures and religions – whether Sikhism, Christianity, Buddhism or Hinduism – talk of the same path to realize God. They agree that there is a way to God and that it lies within each one of us. Some believe we can read scriptures to attune ourselves to the inner realization of the truth, some believe we can pray in whatever customary way we have been taught – burning candles, ringing bells, keeping fasts, praying to the sun or moon. But mystics over the centuries have supported the theory that we are the temple of the living God.

If we accept that God is within us, then there's no need to look outside, no need for idol worship, no need for revering photographs, no need to accumulate knowledge, for, as various saints throughout the ages have said, whatever we get, we will get from within ourselves.

To take our soul to the highest realms, we need to seek him deep within. Everything we seek is inside of us. The journey of the soul is similar to the progress of a seed. Just as we first plant a seed, nurture it, and then benefit from the fruit of the tree, likewise, in spirituality, we need to plant the seed of meditation, nurture it with perseverance and determination, and then experience personally the benefits of our effort. The growth of the seed starts from deep within the earth, while the seed of spirituality starts from deep within the soul.

The taller the tree, the deeper the roots embedded in the earth. So too, in search of spiritual growth, to reach the highest realms of our being, we need to get to the deep core of our inner self. We need to plant the seed of meditation deep within us to reach the higher realms of our consciousness.

But our situation is like that of a story told about Mullah Nasruddin who was searching for something on the ground.

"What have you lost, Mullah?" his friend asked.

"My ring," said the Mullah. So they both bent down on their knees and looked.

After some time the man asked, "Where exactly did you drop it?"

"In my house."

"Then why are you looking here?"

"There is more light here than inside my own house."[6]

That is so like us. We grovel in this world crying to God, "Where are you?" We look for him in temples and churches, in books and idols, while all along, God hides hidden in the hearts of all. He is deep inside of us. As Bulleh Shah wrote:

> bed quraana parrh parrh thakke,
>   sajde kardyaan ghis gaye matthe.
> na rabb teerath na rabb makke,
>   jis paaya tis noor anvaar.

Tired of reading the Vedas and Qur'an,
My forehead was bruised by constant prostration.
God is not at Hindu shrines nor at Muslims' Mecca.
Whosoever found Him,
    found Him within as light divine.[7]

Someone to Show the Way

So now we ask, what next? Where do we go from here? We can't learn through books and discourses, as these can only give us an intellectual insight. We need more! We need a guide, a teacher to direct us because someone has to show the way.

If we were building a house, we would approach an architect for advice. The idea of building a house without the expertise of an architect seems absurd. If we need surgery, we would go to a surgeon. The idea of doing surgery on a patient by anybody other than a surgeon would seem insane. Since each one excels in his or her own specialty, we would take advice from that particular specialist depending on our need. Likewise, when we are in search of God, we would naturally veer towards a person who has attained the ultimate realization of the truth through personal experience.

A sick man visits the doctor for a cure and is administered medicine for his ailment. For us, the Master is the doctor, the disease is separation from the Lord, the medicine is meditation, and we need to take the medication of meditation to cure our separation from the Divine.

In our search for anything in life, we take one step at a time until we gain personal experience. For example, on a child's first day at school, he is hesitant and anxious. The school building, teachers and other children intimidate him. But the next day he is a little more at ease, and as the days and months go by, he finds his comfort level because by then the school building is familiar and the teachers and children are known faces. His experience and familiarity make him more confident and self-assured.

It is the same with our approach to spirituality and the Master. We are afraid at first because the concept is new. The concept seems unfamiliar and even strange. We are eager to know more and yet we are unwilling to take the first step. Our questions indicate our desire for God-realization, yet we find it difficult to head in that direction because the concept is unfamiliar and therefore intimidating. But once we clearly define what we are searching for and understand how to attain the means to that end, our fear slowly gets replaced with eagerness.

There is a moment in our lives when a spark lights within us. We may or may not be searching for spirituality, but knowingly or unknowingly we head in that direction. It is the potentiality that creates a craving within us and draws us to the path. This strong pull and sudden desire is our latent search for truth.

Guru Arjan Dev says:

> sant-sang antar prabh deetha.
> naam prabhu ka laaga meetha.

> In the society of saints,
>   I have seen the Lord within me.
> The Lord's Nam has become sweet unto me.[8]

Do we realize that amongst the billions of people in this world, we have been chosen and given the chance to take advantage of Nam – the path of the divine Sound Current? Kabir Sahib states that the spiritual path is for heroes, not cowards. The road is steep but not impossible! The path is described as being sharper than the edge of a sword.

Guru Nanak says:

bhai re guru bin gyan na ho'e.
poochho brahme naardai bed biaasai ko'e.

O brother, without the Guru,
   divine awakening is not gained.
Know this from Brahma, Narada and Vyas,
   author of the Vedas.[9]

Guru Amar Das says:

gur te boojhai ta dar soojhai.
naam vihoona kath kath loojhai

Through the Guru, if one understands the Lord,
Then he sees the Lord's door.[10]

The concept might be appealing to some and disturbing to others. Some might ask: "Without the Guru? Revere him first to reach the Divine? Can a man just like any one of us be a Master, a Guru, a Saint? Is there such a person as a living Master?" Those questions are inevitable. The theory is so distant and unbelievable, yet so practical, since we need a teacher for everything in life.

Let's understand it in its proper perspective. God chooses not to come to earth but sends his messenger in the human form to connect with us, just as the sun sends out its rays. The ray does not become independent in any way – it is linked to the sun, is a part of the sun, its existence is because of the sun, it has the same qualities as the sun and when the sun sets, the ray merges back with the sun and becomes whole again. The sun's ray is not different from the sun even when it is supposedly away from the sun; it is still connected, its quality remains constant and it remains a part of the whole.

In the same manner, the Master comes to us in the human form. He needs to connect with us on our level of understanding in a way that is appealing and acceptable to us because of the limitations of our mind. Someone with personal experience has to show the way. The Formless assumes the human form to connect with us, and unless we see the Master in his radiant form within, we cannot be assured of his true power – which is why we constantly waver in our faith and trust. We question and doubt because we are not able to stabilize our relationship with the Master's Shabd form – his radiant or spiritual form.

On the physical side, the Master is as human as we are, but herein lies a huge difference: On the spiritual level, he has traversed the path of truth, experienced inner bliss, realized the Ultimate by going deep within himself and being connected to Shabd – the inner spiritual sound. Only a Master has the experience to show us the way within.

No Master, No God!

> I am the Way, the Truth, and the Life.
> Without the Way there is no going;
> Without the Truth there is no Knowing,
> Without the Life, there is no living.
> I am the Way which you must follow;
> The Truth you must believe;
> The Life which you must hope for.[11]
>
> *Thomas à Kempis, Imitation of Christ*

Thomas à Kempis, a medieval monk, explains Christ's teaching:

"I am the Way" – Only a living Master has the key to reveal the "Truth," the way to attain self-realization. Without "Knowing," without personal inner experience, there can be no belief, faith, or attainment. Without "Life" – meaning eternal life or bliss – our liberation, which he calls the "life you must hope for," is not possible. And liberation cannot be attained without someone to show the way.

So Jesus says, "I am the Way" – I have the method to connect you to the path of self-realization, the means to the end, "which you must follow" and practise to attain ultimate bliss, and then Truth will be revealed and believed. "I am the Way" and "without the Way" there is no meaning, no Master, no God.

Similarly, Kabir declares: "Without a Master, none can reach the court of the Lord."[12]

As Guru Nanak taught:

bin satgur kinai na paa'io
bin satgur kinai na paa'ia.

Without the true Guru, no one has obtained the Lord;
without the true Guru, no one ever can.[13]

These words sum up the method or way to our search for spiritual truth, which is through a Master, a Guru. *Gur* means technique or method, and the one that gives the method or technique to attain God is the Guru. Without a Master we are rudderless, living in darkness and ignorance, victims of the five deadly passions of the mind, intricately bound and shackled by *maya* or materialism, stuck in the cycle of birth and death, unable to free ourselves from this worldly bondage, unable to merge with the Absolute because without a Master we cannot attain God.

Yet with the Master, our lives reverse. Through initiation, the Master introduces us to the method or technique of attaining God, of going within ourselves through the practice of meditation, which connects our soul to Shabd, thus permanently removing us from the clutches of birth and death. We are shown the path of divine realization which frees us from worldly bondage. The Master takes us from darkness to light and liberates our soul by merging us with the Absolute, the Ultimate. Such is the power of a Master! Down through the ages, messengers of God, gurus, saints or living Masters like Jesus, Buddha, Mahavira, and Guru Nanak have lived amongst us. They have been ordinary men; they walked and talked like us. But their extraordinary qualities, their realization of the inner truth through personal experience made people revere them as living Masters, saints, or messengers of God.

How did we get our religion, our belief? Hinduism, Christianity, Sikhism, Buddhism, and so forth – from where did these religions surface and how have we inherited them? How do we, after so many centuries, still believe in the past saints and follow their traditions today? Obviously one of our forefathers was a follower of one of the religions of his day and believed in one of the living Masters of that time and hence passed on the tradition to the family. Today these religions persist.

On one hand, we are prepared to believe in the Masters of the past, whom we have no connection with, by praying to them and revering them, with no personal experience of them whatsoever. Yet we are not prepared to apply the same concept today by experiencing it for ourselves with a present living Master. History confirms that there have always been saints or living Masters, throughout human existence. Nothing has changed. As long as man exists, Masters will be there to guide souls back to their ultimate source because there is no other way to attain God-realization.

So Guru Arjan Dev has explained:

> *aapan lee'aa je milai vichhurr kio rovann.*
> *saadhu sang paraapte Nanak rang maanann.*

> If people could meet the Lord by their own efforts,
>   why would they be crying out
>   in the pain of separation?
> Meeting Him in the Saadh Sangat,
>   the company of the Holy,
> O Nanak, celestial bliss is enjoyed.[14]

God by himself is unattainable, God cannot reach his souls, and the souls cannot reach God. Yet through a living Master, God can be attained. Nothing is possible without the Master, yet everything is possible through him. The Master is the means to the end, but there is no end without him. The Master acts as the medium, the link between God and his souls.

The impact of a spiritual guide or exemplar is to extract seekers from their entanglement in external phenomena and take us to the height of spiritual attainment. The Master is supreme, all pervading and all encompassing. He is the focal point, the centre and the nucleus. The Master is the key to the door of existence. The entire universe is concentrated in him.

For those who have connected to the Master's Shabd form, who have seen his radiant form, have had the inner experience, they know there is no difference between the Master and God; they perceive the Master and God as one, not separate, but a part of the whole – like the sun and its ray – the same Shabd, the same energy, the same power, the same consciousness.

Personal experience reveals that the first truth is the Master, then God. No Master, no God!

Spiritual Awakening

Just as we cannot cook without a fire or light a room with a photograph of a light bulb, in our search for spirituality, we need the right connection, someone who can light that spark within us, to show us the light. That connection – our spiritual awakening – is initiation.

During initiation the Master introduces the method of meditation that connects the seeker to the Word, Logos or Shabd. What is transmitted to us during initiation is the direct experience of the wisdom of the Master, who embodies complete realization of inner truth. The Masters put their knowledge and experience into their teachings, the spiritual treasury of their inner wisdom. Through their teachings they show us how to merge the soul back to its source. And through their experience they assure us that only through meditation can ultimate truth be revealed to us. Although a true Master has both the knowledge and experience of God, he only imparts his knowledge to us. We need to experience the way and the truth for ourselves, through meditation.

The initiation of a disciple into Sant Mat and the practice of meditation does not restrict the seeker from following his own religion. The teachings stand above the barriers of caste, creed and nationality.

Neither does initiation guarantee us health and wealth. If achieving riches were the criterion for spirituality, then Jesus and Buddha must have been spiritual failures in such a book of rules. Jesus had no material prosperity. Buddha relinquished all he had. And so has it been with many other mystics.

The Zen Buddhist saying "Study the living word, not the dead word" embodies the true teachings of religion and philosophy. Dead words are what we learn from books and scriptures; they give superficial knowledge, knowledge without experience. Books can give us information, they can motivate and inspire us, but they cannot give us experience.

In books we read stories and anecdotes, and we find them beautiful. But more beautiful than words is personal experience. Words are not essential for attaining inner truth; we require the mind to be silenced during meditation, so what good is book knowledge? To experience inner truth, we don't need encyclopaedias and PhD's. We need the living word, not the dead word.

The Bible says, "Except a man be born again, he cannot see the kingdom of God."[15] Being "born again" refers to initiation; that is our rebirth. We are reborn through spiritual awakening, through which we can see the kingdom of God when we cease to identify ourselves with our body and realize ourselves as spirit.

Only an illumined teacher, a living Master, can transmit the word of God to us through initiation. Initiation is a mystical spark bestowed by a living Master to his disciples, thus igniting their dormant spiritual energy. Once lit, its fire keeps burning when the five names (simran) are constantly repeated.

Through initiation the Master dehypnotizes us from the illusions of this materialistic world and awakens us from our deep slumber and shows us the way to the Divine. We need to meditate constantly on the power of simran given to us by the Master.

The process of meditation is compared to the mythological story of the formation of the pearl, as told by Sri Ramakrishna Paramahansa: "When the rain falls, the oyster opens its shell and collects a drop of water. Then it dives down to the seabed and remains there till the raindrop is converted into a beautiful pearl."[16]

In the same way, after we receive the power of simran from the Master, only one-pointed zeal can turn us towards the pearl of spiritual illumination.

Role of a Master

je sau chanda ugvah sooraj charrah hajaar,
ete chaanan hodiaan gur bin ghor andhaar.

If a hundred moons were to rise,
    and a thousand suns appeared –
    even with such light,
    there would still be pitch darkness
    without the Guru.[17]

                             Guru Angad Dev

Even if a thousand suns were to shine, we would remain in utter darkness and ignorance without a spiritual Master. There is no salvation without a Master.

The Master's role is to remind us of the teachings and bring our attention to a greater perception and realization, back to the root of spirituality through meditation, which is the fundamental practice of our inner quest. He teaches the technique which connects the disciple's soul to the inner self through concentration. He teaches us how to focus the mind and contemplate on the form of the Master through dhyan.

The teachings are straightforward – God-realization through meditation. We are shown the way to liberation through the method taught at initiation, which releases us from the cycle of birth and death. The crucial choice of how easy or difficult we make it for ourselves is left to us and whether choose to practise or not practise what we've been taught, because just as we cannot walk towards the north and south at the same time, we cannot live in both freedom and bondage!

The Master is the indispensable link between the disciple and liberation. The Master's inner knowledge provides a window through which the disciple can grasp the teachings. The Master weeds the disciple's mind by replanting awareness.

The Master-disciple relationship is intricately woven with trust and faith. He is our redeemer. Although at the beginning we may think of him as our father, brother, friend, or beloved, ultimately those words do not describe or define the intensity and purity of the unique bond between the Master and disciple. Only this relationship is truly real. It is deep, strong, and everlasting!

The Master persistently drills home the fact that we should not worship the physical but reach out for the spiritual. We just don't get it – we continue to frolic in inane activities like sending emails and text messages to exchange news of the Master. One question we ask, for example, is "How long did he sit for satsang?" We focus on the quantity, not what we gained from his presence. Not the substance of what he said but only the length of time he sat. We get into frivolous details about what he wears or how he walks, how he looks and how he talks, What does it matter if he wears a turban, a hat or neither, whether he has a beard or not, if he chooses to wear a kurta pyjama or just hang out in a pair of jeans and a sweatshirt?

These are mere outward trappings and have no spiritual significance. These do not determine the depth, purity or significance of the Master's spiritual power and purpose amongst us. These things clutter our minds taking us further away from reality and the truth.

We remain stubbornly stagnant in the misconception that worshipping and chasing the physical form of the Master will compensate for lack of spiritual practice. If the Master's efforts to ingrain in us the need to work towards our goal are falling on deaf ears, then we're in deep trouble. If, after all this, we do not follow the only *hukam* – the only real command he gives – self-realization and God-realization through the technique of meditation, then we have reached a dead end.

We need to hear the Master's message which is loud and clear: there is no substitute for meditation. Just like there is no way to satisfy hunger except by eating food, there is no way for us connect with the divinity within except through meditation.

Baba Ji explains explicitly that dependence on the physical form of the Master can become a hindrance in our inner journey.

The physical form guides, inspires and motivates us towards our inward journey but is not the end goal in our spiritual quest. We need to channelize the precious energy and power received from the physical form and translate it to inner devotion and dedication.

The power of love for the physical should persuade us to move inwards to connect with the radiant form. If we stop at the physical, our inner growth will stagnate.

The physical form is the gateway to our spiritual journey, but the formless is our ultimate goal. We tend to satisfy the mind by claiming that physical darshan is a substitute for meditation. We justify this attitude with stories of the saints' desperate desire for physical darshan of their Master.

For example, after Baba Jaimal Singh left the physical plane, the Great Master said: *"Je meinu Baba Ji Maharaj aa ke darshan dein, taan mein apna sab kuch michavar karen nu tayar haan,"* meaning: "I would sacrifice everything if Baba Jaimal Singh Ji

Maharaj would give me his darshan."[18] The Great Master was expressing his yearning and longing for his Master's physical darshan.

First a disciple is drawn to the physical form of a Master and then slowly begins to love the physical form to a point that drives him to desperate longing and yearning for more. His desire becomes more intense to go within and experience the Shabd form. Once he has seen and experienced the radiant or Shabd form, the disciple realizes the significance of the physical form. But if a disciple stops only at the physical, if he does not experience the radiant form, he cannot truly understand and absorb the significance of the physical form of the Master.

The Great Master had experienced the radiant form, so he knew the true value of his Master's darshan. His deep, intense craving for physical darshan was an extension of his inner experience. So here, a realized disciple, the Great Master, is expressing the priceless value of the physical darshan of his Master, after having seen the Master's Shabd form. This passion and fervour comes from a different level altogether.

But we haven't reached that level, so we can't apply the Great Master's experience to our own journey Our craving for darshan must not stop at the physical if we want to experience the same intensity and deep love as the Great Master for his Master's physical darshan. We would have to go through the same inner experience.

Hazur Maharaj Charan Singh further explains: "May your love of the form culminate in the love of the Formless."[19]

Hazur clearly and lovingly expresses that the culmination of our inner journey is attaching ourselves to the Formless – the

Shabd form of the Master. Love for the physical form is a stepping stone to the Formless, which is the goal and purpose of our spiritual journey.

Baba Ji expresses the same thought when he says that we insist on looking for the physical form on the inside and the astral form outside. Baba Ji explains: Don't stop at the physical – that is not the end – move on, move inwards, allow our love to motivate us to connect with the radiant form. The physical form is not the ultimate aim or intention of our spiritual journey; it is the beginning, the start, the appetizer. He wants us to translate that intense love of the physical into effort to reach the Formless. The role of the Master is to ensure that our love for the physical culminates in reaching the Formless.

Traits of a True Master

When a disciple asked his teacher what the sign of a real Guru is, he replied, "It is not his form, it is not his appearance, it is not what he says; it is his atmosphere, it is what his presence conveys to you, what his atmosphere tells you."[20]

An enlightened Master is merged in his supreme self; he is connected to the Shabd within – he is exclusively committed to the teachings in thought, word and action. His mind is replete with every quality of realization. The sharpened perception that a Master attains takes him to unprecedented heights of self-revelation, which enables him to experience things that are imperceptible to others. The Master lives above the level of the ego, the self, the "I" – therefore he lives merged in complete bliss.

We often refer to a Master as a "perfect living Master"– perfection here refers to his internal vision of truth. This truth is not a result of intellectual speculation but of practical realization. This truth is not born of rituals and dogmas but of personal experience. Because of this personal experience, the Master remains in the realm of higher consciousness therefore he is naturally unattached and free from material senses and contamination.

A true Master remains untouched by anger even when he appears to be so. He is detached even though he may seem involved with family and friends. He remains detached even though he may possess wealth, and he has no pride even though he has a tremendous following.

He does not get disheartened at criticism but remains open-minded. However exhausted he may be physically or mentally, he continues his spiritual work with love and patience. His conduct is flawless and he is unstained by negative emotions. He is totally committed to pure thought, word and action. The Master is an embodiment of love, wisdom, forgiveness, compassion and selfless dedication to mankind.

True saints do not take a fee for imparting spiritual knowledge. They earn their own livelihood, reject gifts, discourage obeisance from disciples, and avoid performing miracles. As Henry Hamblin, an early twentieth-century English mystic, wrote about the true spiritual teacher: "...that on no account a charge be demanded for revealing spiritual truths and that all money received by the teacher be regarded as God's and used accordingly."[21]

A perfect example is the Dera's use of donated funds: Everything received in donation is carefully and purposefully used for the sangat – for food, accommodation and other facilities. Dera has been built with the sangat's love for the Master and the Master's love for the sangat.

A true Master does not ask for our wealth, rather he is waiting to share the immeasurable treasure he has. He is not interested in our riches; he wants to enrich us with the inner wealth he possesses as a result of his inner experience.

A Master doesn't advertise for seekers to join his flock; he advises them to understand the principles of the path before embarking on their spiritual journey by asking for initiation.

A true Master has imbibed all the necessary attributes, and through his inner experience he transmits the teachings – his primary task is to initiate seekers and teach them the method of spiritual practice.

A Master cannot be judged merely by how he acts outwardly. His outward actions, his joys or pains, or his intellectual knowledge cannot alter or affect his bliss within, because he dwells in divine ecstasy even while in the human form.

The Master exudes a mysterious power, an uncanny authority and an abundance of grace. Just being in his presence, the atmosphere is charged with his magnetism. Sitting before him, we slowly start to fall in tune with him – on some level we connect with his divinity. When we sit before a true Master we feel an infectious joy and peace. We allow that feeling to radiate and engulf us, letting it overflow to the people around us, who share in the love that fills us with such joy.

That intoxicating joy is a direct gift from the divinity radiating from the Master!

The First Truth

A story is told about the Indian saint, Kabir Sahib:

Kabir was perplexed when faced with God and his Master. He wondered: To whom should I bow first? Then he said:

> *guru gobind dou kharre, ka ke laagaun paanye*
> *balihaari guru apne, jin gobind diyo bataaye.*

> Should the Lord and my Guru appear together,
>   at whose feet should I then prostrate myself?
> I sacrifice myself to my own Guru,
>   for he is the one who revealed the Lord to me.[22]

Profound words!

The Master and God are one, but for the disciple the Master comes before God because the Master is the means to God. It's the Master who initiates the disciple, who opens the door to the inner worlds for the disciple. The Master is the password, the door to the kingdom of heaven, so the disciple has to acknowledge the Master first.

Only after the disciple has passed through the door of the Master can he face God. If the door is closed, there is nowhere to enter.

So first the Master, then God!

The Master is the means to God; he is the source; he is all-important to the disciple – without him nothing is possible, so that's why Kabir Sahib says, "I have to touch my Master's feet first."

In the scriptures and poetry of the saints, the Masters are looked upon with high regard, utmost respect, and greatest reverence; it is often difficult to distinguish whether they are talking of the Master or God.

The Master is the truth, and that is the truth about the Master!

Blissful Delusions

Clouds of Illusion

Truth is simple, illusion makes it infinitely intricate.[23]

Meher Baba

When something is simple, we often find it difficult to accept. The mind goes into overdrive wondering how it can be so simple. There must be a catch, a trick we've missed. Our mind has the knack of making simple things complicated.

However, if a situation is complicated, the mind revels in the complexity; yet it grumbles that the problem should be simpler. The human mind makes simple things complicated and complicated things even more complex.

We revel in illusions. Is it a form of escapism, of refuting the reality by running away from it, unable to face the truth head-on? Or is it lack of understanding?

We run to palmists and astrologers to know our future – but who can predict what will happen the next moment in our lives, let alone ten years hence? We have probably heard the story of an astrologer who predicted other people's futures but didn't know that his own daughter would be widowed.

Palmists may predict that we will be wealthy and live till a ripe old age, but the next day an earthquake can bury our family and its wealth in just a few moments.

Illusions stem from fear!

Fear of the unknown, fear of death, fear of living, fear of acceptance, fear of rejection, fear of illness, fear of poverty, and fear of fear itself. We are gripped with fear – so we comfort ourselves with illusions by creating myths as a form of escape from reality.

How often have we watched the clouds lazily pass over us in the sky – each individual draws his own conclusion about its shape, and even while we are visualizing the shape, it continuously changes. The shapes the clouds form are illusions and eventually evaporate into nothingness. Our lives and relationships, wealth and poverty, happiness and sadness are the same – merely illusions. As we watch them, they slowly evaporate into nothingness.

Shakespeare wrote, "All the world's a stage, and all the men and women merely players."[24]

The world is the sky and the players are the clouds that roll by in different shapes, only to vanish into nothingness. But truth is simple. Truth is permanent.

And the only way to truth is to go within, where we have to go alone, in an ego-less state, in love, in silence, in concentration, in yearning and in believing!

Truth is that simple!

Only Four Births After Initiation

We console ourselves with misinterpretations of what we read in the Sant Mat literature – the most bizarre being that once we are initiated, we will have at most only four births. This is a huge misconception!

The Great Master is quoted as having said that after initiation, "it takes no more than four births."[25]

Yes, the Master really said that!

It is easy for us to misunderstand the words of a Master because our perspective is limited. The Master's words are loaded with a depth and intensity – a divinity – way beyond our comprehension!

Masters express themselves in various ways at different times to reach out to the people of their time, but the message itself remains constant. Masters from different eras express their message in their unique ways.

The Master refers to our life after initiation as a meditative life – a life in which we follow his instructions to meditate every day and live strictly within the other vows we take. Look at the implicit trust the Master places in his disciples: he takes it on faith that once initiated, his disciples will naturally turn their lives around from a materialistic life and channel it to a meditative life, a spiritual life. He doesn't doubt our eagerness and intention. He believes in us. So he says that once initiated, when we live in meditation, only then, after a maximum of four lives, can we attain liberation and reach Sach Khand.

We need to grasp his meaning: By meditation, he doesn't mean us sitting on a cushion watching the clock and doing mechanical simran once in a while.

Just being initiated does not guarantee God-realization and spiritual liberation within four lives. We have to steep ourselves in meditation. If just the act of being initiated would guarantee liberation, then why do the Masters persistently remind us to meditate?

If initiation alone were the key to salvation, then why bother to wake up at the unearthly hour at 3:00 am? Why go through the torture of sitting still for two and a half hours every day?

Initiation is merely the means – meditation is the end! Being in a "meditative state" for four lifetimes will ensure our salvation, not just receiving initiation. Meditation is the only solution and the only way.

If we have a key to the door of our house, sticking the key in our pocket and expecting the door to open magically is foolishness. We need to insert the key in the lock for it to open. If a doctor prescribes medicine for an ailment and we purchase the medicine but don't take it, it certainly won't cure our ailment. We may possess a book, but if we don't read it, it is wasted – it remains just a possession. The action of reading would benefit us, not merely possession of the book.

It's the same with initiation. We need to put the initiation into action by meditating; if we don't, the initiation is wasted.

We have the remarkable ability to create convenient concepts and twist them into innovative interpretations – but that doesn't make them true.

Swami Vivekananda said: "Even the *devas* (gods) will have to come down again and attain salvation through the human body."[26]

And Kabir said:

is dehi kau simrah dev.
so dehi bhaj har ki sev.

This body even the *devas* long to acquire.
So through this body of thine,
    perform thou devoted service to the Lord.[27]

Profound words! Even the *devas* have to be born in the human form to attain salvation. The human form is supreme! Through the human form we have the ability to meditate, which cleanses and purifies our soul. The one and only criterion for removing ourselves from the cycle of existence is through meditation.

No Return to the Animal Kingdom

The Master is also quoted as having said that after initiation we will not go back to the animal kingdom.

Yes, the Master has said that too!

But Hazur Maharaj Ji made it amply clear: "If we refuse to behave like humans, if we have made up our mind and are determined to behave like animals, then where is the justification to get the human form? We have to go down."[28]

These chilling words from Hazur should put aside any arguments we may have on this subject.

Our misinterpretations, no matter how soothing and comforting, cannot alter the fact that our actions or karmas will determine whether we return in the human form or are thrown back to the animal kingdom. The kingdom we are reborn into is determined by the nature of our actions and the state of consciousness resulting from those actions. We are trapped within the vicious cycle of rebirth according to our karmas. As the Buddha explains:

> As the seed, so the fruit.
> Whoever does good, receives good.
> Whoever does bad, receives bad.[29]

The consequence of "bad" has to be endured, as that is the karmic fate in the grander scheme of cause and effect.

Our misunderstanding of the Master's words would give us carte blanche to commit murders, adultery, robberies and so forth and yet stand vindicated – which implies that once initiated, the law of karma gets nullified and we can happily commit crimes as we skip along in life yet be reassured of a human birth. What a way to go! We live in a fool's paradise if we remotely believe this to be true.

In karma theory, no action goes unrewarded or unpunished; we are continuously swept along by the cycle of karmas. An anonymous verse expresses this:

> Sow a thought and reap a deed
> Sow a deed and reap a habit
> Sow a habit and reap a character
> Sow a character and reap a destiny.

We reap our destiny through our actions. We pay for every thought, word and action as per the unquestionable laws laid down by the universe. None of our wild illusions can remove the harsh fact that we have to burn the seeds of karmas individually.

In the human world we are governed by norms set by society for social acceptance, regulations for right and wrong, rules for misconduct, laws governing crimes committed. Each of our actions results in consequences, whether one is ostracized by society for social misbehaviour, punished for breaking regulations or for violating norms of misconduct, or for outright criminal activities. Each of these actions has reactions. Each individual has to go through the consequences of his actions. Negative actions and evil deeds can toss us back into the lower realms – that is the consequence of the karmic debacle, the principle of the cosmic law of nature: "Whatever a man sows, that he shall also reap."[30]

This precious human birth is powerful and extremely purposeful. Those who have been initiated by a true Master into the meditation practice will cross the ocean of boundless and unfathomable suffering and attain liberation. This opportunity is rare and unique and should not be squandered; it should spur us on to go inwards and upwards through our spiritual practice.

Six Months of Meditation Ensures Enlightenment

It is also said that the Master assures us that we can be enlightened if we meditate for six months.[31]

Yes, the Master has really said this too!

The Master's definition of meditation and our interpretation are distinctly different.

We draw our conclusions according to what we are capable of understanding. For us, meditation is sitting in the required position and dozing off in slumber-land, or having wandering thoughts about the next movie to watch or the next destination to visit on vacation.

To the Master, "six months of meditation" clearly means that during meditation, if our attention is focussed at the eye centre with no thought, totally centred, that would assure us enlightenment. Are we able to do that? Can we claim that during meditation we are able to focus our attention and exclude all other thoughts? And have we been able to maintain that focus consistently for six months? The foundation of simran and bhajan has to be very deep, steady, and continuous for the focus to be centred and anchored at the eye centre.

The Master's assurance lies in the simplicity of his words. The complexity lies in our interpretation. The Masters never mince their words, while we never fail to misunderstand them.

Initiation doesn't guarantee us salvation; initiation gives us the technique. But having this knowledge does not give us the required results because knowing is not attaining. Knowing is the beginning, the seed, the route to the centre – reaching the centre comes only through practice, and practice results in attainment.

Socrates was declared the wisest man in the world. People ran to give him the news. Socrates responded, "Go and tell them that I know nothing. How can I be the wisest man in the world?" The people were shocked, and out of curiosity they went back to find out what the oracle would say. The oracle laughed and said, "Because he has come to a point of realizing that he knows nothing; that makes him the wisest man in the world."

When we shed the baggage of knowledge, when the mind rests in nothingness, then we can truly know.

A Chinese proverb puts it very simply: "I hear and I forget, I see and I remember, I do and I understand."

It is the same with initiation: doing is the key.

The length of time we practise meditation does not determine our progress or guarantee results. It's not important how many years we have been initiated but how diligently we have practised.

We cannot attain the truth without breaking the walls of ignorance with continuous practice. Only relentless effort, daily practice, and focus can achieve results. Time here is meaningless!

Teachings Are Greater than the Master

A Master would often repeat at the end of his discourse: "Remove the self, and realize truth."

The disciple was compelled to ask him one day: "Master, if this is so, why don't you remove the self for us and just explain the pure truth?"

The Master smiled and asked the disciple to get him water to drink.

The disciple brought a glass of water and placed it in front of the Master.

"What is this?" asked the Master.

"This is the water you asked for," murmured the disciple.

"But did I ask for a glass or water?"

The disciple was confused.

"Never mind," the Master explained softly. "Just as you cannot bring water without a vessel, so too, the Master is required to express the truth through the teachings."[32]

The teachings are of paramount importance – they were then, are now, and will remain so – even a thousand years from today!

The teachings remain constant, but the Masters change – yet the teachings can be taught only by the Master.

Now let's get a deeper clarity on this.

In every era there is a Master to show the way to the truth. When one Master leaves the physical plane, another succeeds him, because it is imperative to have a Master to teach the truth. So even though the Masters continue to change, they continue to teach the same truth because there is only one truth.

The teachings cannot manifest in disciples by themselves; that is like trying to bring water without a glass. It is impossible.

A glass is essential to hold water. Water needs a glass, a container, a vessel, a stream, a river, or an ocean – it cannot contain itself by itself. The teachings too, cannot contain themselves without a Master.

The Master is the glass, the container, the vessel; he holds the water and dispenses the water. The Master is the custodian of the teachings because of his inner experience. The Master is the glass holding the teachings and only he can teach the truth.

So the Master and teachings cannot be separated. They are bound together, they are inseparable. Teachings cannot be taught without the Master and the Master cannot teach without the experience of truth.

The Master is not greater than the truth, and truth is not greater than the Master – they are blended into one, merged into a whole. It's like the water and the enormous pit that holds the water – together they are called an ocean. There is no ocean if the pit and the water are separated, but together they form a mighty ocean. Without each other they are incomplete. In the same way, the Master and the teachings cannot be separated – they are the ocean, they are merged together, they are one blended from two!

Perception of a Master

It is essential to understand that our faith should not be based on the Master's human form. Nor can we indulge in the belief that the Master has come down from heaven to wave a magic wand so that we can have our worldly cravings granted and live happily ever after. The myths we build around the Master's physical form and actions come from our imagination. We conjure up illusions that the Master is here to protect us from sickness and death, to make us rich and famous, to erase our karmas, to fulfil our materialistic desires, and to advise us on our worldly life. We expect the Master to be a magician, doctor, stockbroker, marriage counsellor, and an astrologer all rolled into one.

And talking of astrologers, let's see the end value of their skill. A Greek astrologer was studying the stars at night, missed a step and fell into a well. An old woman heard his screams and ran to pull him out.

Gratefully he said, "I am a famous astrologer, come to my office tomorrow and I will tell you your future for free as you have saved my life."

The old woman laughed: "You can't see one step ahead and tumbled straight into the well, so how can you predict my future?"

We tend to desperately hold on to the fictitious image we have created about the Master and deliberately invent illusions about him because we expect he will then be compelled to prove himself. We first test him by putting him on a pedestal and award him fancy names and titles – but when we are disillusioned, we drag him down from the same pedestal. When things go our way, we feel him with us and within us and we use multitudes of adjectives to describe his greatness, grace, kindness, and compassion. But like the Ferris wheel that goes up and then comes down, when we feel low, we suddenly see him turn dispassionate from compassionate, unkind from kind, and small from great.

We deviate completely from the track – if we're not chasing the physical form or expecting miracles, we're bringing our personal problems to the Master. We request interviews and write letters, asking inane questions about family matters, how to solve our property disputes, what career our son should choose, or what business to start. We offload ourselves hoping to get answers so we can have someone to blame if things go wrong, or we announce boastfully that a miracle has been performed if all goes well.

Here's a story about blame. One day Mullah Nasruddin's house got burgled. There was commotion everywhere. His wife blamed him, accusing him of not locking the door. The neighbours blamed him for leaving the windows open. Everyone was blaming Mullah.

Then he screamed: "One minute please, I am not to blame."

The neighbours asked, "Then who is to blame?"

Mullah replied, "What about the thief?"[33]

That is our situation. We want someone to blame. We don't want to take responsibility for our own actions. It is easier for the mind to blame someone else, because then the burden is off our shoulders and on the other person's.

We also attach miracles to the Master if one of our loved ones is saved in an accident. What about the other who died? Was the Master partial to one and not the other? Think about this – which was the real miracle – for the one who died or the one who survived? We have a worldly relationship with our loved ones, only till the cremation ground – that's where our relationship ends. After that, there is no father, mother, sister, brother, husband, wife, or child. The Master does not guarantee that we will not face death, pain, and other human frailties. As a matter of fact, we are constantly being prepared for this very death we dread so much.

We may use our perception to judge the Master's words and actions, but he works according to his perception, whether his actions seem right or wrong to us. Our inadequate understanding will not deter him from doing what he is here to do. The problem is really with us – it's our lack of faith that makes us question everything he does and says.

When we see the Master in the human form, we judge his words and actions – nothing unique, that's the fabric of human nature. But since we are limited, we tend to limit the Master too. That is exactly why the Master constantly warns us not to attach ourselves to the physical. On the physical level there is instability, impermanence and inconsistency, which rock the balance in our mind, creating upheaval in our lives. We often choose the path of ignorance because we tend to cling to the phantoms of the physical, instead of striving to achieve something higher that is not subject to change and decay.

Our concepts and illusions about the Master are human-based, restricted due to our lack of understanding, lack of faith, and lack of awareness. We envision the Master from a narrow perspective thereby limiting his presence and purpose in our lives.

We cannot understand the Master's ways, why he does what he does – he is unfathomable, unexplainable, indefinable and incomprehensible. That is the enigma of the Master; we need faith to accept what we do not understand. We need to let go of trying to judge the Master from our limited human perspective.

So let's be clear and leave no room for ambiguity: the Master is a spiritual guide!

Embracing Rites and Rituals

The Master has gone to extreme lengths to tear us away from rites and rituals. He intentionally wants us to break away from these illusions and myths and concentrate on the reality.

The well opposite the Great Master's *kothi* (house) was made inaccessible and we were jolted out of our stupor. The well was built with the sole aim of providing water, but we turned it into a well of "divine nectar," carrying bottles of "holy" water home to heal people or transform them into our belief.

A story is told about Guru Nanak. The Guru was watching a group of men bathing in the Ganges. He saw them pouring water towards the sun and asked: "What is it that you are doing?"

They answered, "We are sending water to the sun."

Hearing this, Guru Nanak stepped into the Ganges and started pouring water in the opposite direction.

The men were aghast. "What are you doing?"

Guru Nanak replied calmly: "I am sending water to my fields in Kartarpur – they are in this direction."

"How can the water reach your fields in Kartarpur?"

Guru Nanak said innocently: "If your water can reach the sun, then my fields are much closer."[34]

We would say the men were crazy to believe the water would reach the sun, but then we are equally crazy to believe that water from a well is divine nectar. The entire Dera has been built by the Masters, so how do we decide which part is sacred and which isn't? These are rituals the Master wants us to drop so that we can move on to our search for truth.

Bhandaras were discontinued because they became an excuse for pilgrimages to the Dera, as the dates coincided with the previous Masters' birth or death anniversaries. We need to drop these traditions. Sant Mat is a path which is deeply committed to our inward journey, not outer rituals.

Satsang ghar tours were discontinued because we were paying homage to the building. Baba Ji has cautioned that if we continue bowing to the satsang ghar, he would not hesitate to tear the building down. Traditionally, shrines were built in different places so people could use their quietness in remembrance of the Lord and to practise meditation. But we turned these into "holy" buildings. Instead of praying inside them, we started praying to them. We are urged to listen to the sound inside and see the light with our inner eyes, but it seems easier to take a shortcut and ring bells and light candles outside. These rituals are not a solution because there are no shortcuts. These rituals just hinder our spiritual progress.

The Master changed his title from Maharaj Ji to Baba Ji to break our habit of using the more traditional title. He used his changed appearance during his recent illness to tear us away from idolizing the physical form, with the deliberate intention of making us search for him within. What other lengths need the Master go to for us to understand his simple message?

These steps are taken to bring our attention back to the simplicity of the teachings, to retain the essence of Sant Mat teachings by focussing on the journey within, to stop Sant Mat from turning ritualistic or becoming another religion.

Sant Mat is a spiritual path and will forever remain so without the crutches of rites and rituals.

We leave one myth and latch on to another. The Master is here to tear us away from myths, rites, and rituals – to kill them completely, to demolish them and bring our focus back to the simplicity of the teachings.

Being Closer Means Better Darshan

This is a huge fallacy; we cage the Master's power because of our ignorance. We restrict his power by believing he is a human body sitting on stage, and think that the closer we are, the better the darshan will be. We are so far off from the truth.

Take the sun for instance; it is not limited to a particular continent or country. The sun has tremendous power to shower its radiance, energy, and light to the entire world. The stars and moon are completely shadowed in its presence and the absence of the sun creates utter darkness. That is the unique power of the sun.

If we lock ourselves in a room and close the windows, we will not benefit from the sun's warmth and light. We need to draw back the curtains, open the doors and windows and let the sunshine pour in or be outside to bask in the glory of the sun. Either way, the sun will continue to shed its radiance; whether we are receptive to it or not is up to us.

Like the sun, the Master sends out his power and radiance everywhere equally, it isn't stronger in front and weaker at the back of a pandal or hall. We need to be receptive. Just as we cannot sit in a room and complain that we are not feeling the sun's warmth, if we are not meditating, we will not be able to absorb the radiance of the Master. The Master's power is constantly present if we remain receptive to it and don't shut our doors.

We cannot fathom the Master's power with these physical eyes. We can't look directly at the sun – it would blind us – yet we can enjoy its warmth and light by being in its presence. Here too, we can enjoy the blissful warmth of the Master's radiance with these outer eyes, but we will remain ignorant of his true power, which can be revealed only through meditation, if we don't practise.

That is why Baba Ji repeatedly says that we cannot "take" darshan; it is "given" to us. The sun's light continues to shine whether we look at the sun or not. In the same way, the Master's power and energy flow everywhere equally. Whether we sit in front or at the back is not important because his power resonates all over. But to experience the full impact of the Master's darshan and radiance we need to make ourselves receptive by living in his *hukam*, by living a meditative way of life.

The Master's aura and power are unlimited and infinite. But if we fail to see his radiance, it's because we restrict him to a human form.

Only a jeweller knows the real value of a diamond, only a mother understands her love for her child, only a farmer knows the preciousness of his crop.

Likewise, only those who meditate know the true value of the Master's darshan.

Speakers Are Elevated Souls

Some of us have a misconception that satsang speakers are elevated souls.

Speakers are not chosen because they are more intelligent, knowledgeable or elevated. Their knowledge comes from satsangs and books; they repeat the teachings from the Master's discourses, other satsangs or information gathered from books. Speakers are ordinary sevadars like the rest of us. Speakers struggle just as much as anyone else. They experience the normal bouts of doubts and fears like us. Their faith too gets shaky like ours. For who is there who does not waver from time to time?

There is no difference in any kind of seva we do, for all seva is equal. We cannot compare one seva to another. We know that seva is not given because of a special skill or talent one might have. There are people from all walks of life doing all kinds of seva: The vice chancellor of a university did seva in the fruit stall; doctors do *mitti* (dirt-carrying) seva, high-ranking officials serve food in the langar, army officers wash dishes in the kitchens, teachers and professors do seva in the sanitation department, judges and lawyers serve as ushers at satsang, and so on. Seva is given to us according to our need, as seen by the Master.

Speakers' egos can be a grave concern. An attitude that they are better than the rest of the sangat is detrimental to them. Seva done with ego nullifies the effect of that seva. Also, the belief that speakers are role models is a charade; they are erring mortals like us and do not receive special divine status by being speakers. It is easier to write and speak about the teachings than to practise them. Consciously or unconsciously, speakers often highlight issues during their talks that they themselves struggle with. Nothing wrong with that! But giving satsang does not elevate their status in any way.

Speakers can give us a new, fresh perspective. They explain their understanding of the teaching. They put across their point of view, a fresh idea, another form of expression, a different method of explanation, which gives us food for thought. We look for different points of view when choosing books on a particular subject. We feel the need to enhance our understanding and knowledge by reading about other views. One way of explanation may not appeal to some but may be very meaningful to another. It is the same with satsang speakers; they bring their form of expression in different, refreshing ways to inspire and motivate us on the path of God-realization.

The teachings remain unchanged. It should not be assumed that a satsang given by a speaker is based on his or her inner experiences. Generally, their talk is a repetition of the teachings they have heard or read, being expressed in their own manner. In all probability, those with inner experiences might not be able to speak.

The only one who can be a true teacher is one who has experienced truth himself, the one who is all knowing.

The Master's satsangs are the highest form of teachings. They are totally authentic – through his discourses we get indisputable learning, knowledge, wisdom, inspiration, and motivation because he expresses the truth from his inner experiences. The Master is the teachings personified.

The VIP Syndrome

VIP is a "very important person" – who amongst us would dare come forward to claim that title?

First of all, what are the qualities required to be "important" on a spiritual path?

The answer to this is simple – none!

The word "important" is nonexistent in the dictionary of spirituality because it is starkly opposite of the teachings. A spiritual path is about losing the identity, surrendering the ego, killing the "I." Spirituality does not recognize "important" people – rather it crushes their importance. There is only one way to heaven: to break the mountainous ego into rubble and pound the rubble into mud. The doorway to spirituality is closed to boulders and rubble; only soft mud can pass through. We need to crush our sense of importance into mud. The "I" is a mountain; it cannot stand up to the journey within, it contains too much baggage. Only when the ego is deflated, when one is crushed into mud, can the inner doors open and the journey begin.

Secondly, many of us believe that we are important if we hold certain positions. Here is a humorous commentary on the delusion of our self-importance:

The brain said, since I control everything and do all the work, I should be boss.

The feet said, since I carry man where he wants to go and get him to do what the brain wants, I should be boss.

The hands said, since I must do all the work and earn all the money to keep all the rest of you going, I should be boss.

The eyes said, since I must look out for all of you and tell you where danger lurks, I should be boss.

And so it went with the heart, ears, and lungs.

Finally the rectum spoke up and demanded that he be boss. All the other parts laughed at the idea of him being boss.

The rectum was so angered that he blocked himself and refused to function. Soon the brain was feverish, the eyes crossed and ached, the feet were too weak to walk, the hands hung limply, and heart and lungs struggled to survive.

Finally they all pleaded with the brain to relent and let the rectum be boss, and so it happened. All parts did their work and the rectum bossed and relieved himself.

So, who was the boss? None of them! It's teamwork! Positions may seem important, some may believe their departments or centres will fall apart without them, but we can be transferred, retire, resign, or die. The seva will continue as usual. That is how unimportant we are in the big picture. The focus should be on creating a harmonious, congenial atmosphere that will make us realize the futility of self-importance.

Third, we often believe that giving donations makes us VIPs.

In the book *Treasure Beyond Measure*, Hazur gives an example of a satsangi with one leg who used to come during bhandaras:

He used to come from the hills of Himachal and was very poor. Just to save money to give in seva, he used to walk from his village in the hills to the Dera, with the help of his crutches, covering a distance of over seventy-five miles. Once he was brought to me.... He offered one rupee in seva. Looking to his poverty, I asked the sevadars not to accept it, but he burst into tears and I had to accept his offering.

How can you value this seva? Is it not worth much more than the hundreds and thousands that the rich give? The value of seva is not in how much one offers, but in the feelings and love with which it is offered.[35]

Donation given with a motive ceases to be a donation. It's a transaction; we're trying to make a deal.

Look around and see how the sharing, caring nature of people has changed over the years, even at Dera. When there were only small houses, people had big hearts. They opened their homes and hearts to family and friends. They spread mattresses wherever they could for them to sleep and ate whatever was cooked. There was a great sense of loving and belonging. There were hardly any guest houses or hostels then, so people helped each other and had to make do.

Today the houses have become bigger, but the hearts have often become smaller. Brothers, sisters, nieces and nephews are no longer as welcome in relatives' homes. They are now termed "guests," not "family." Even here, as in the rest of the world, materialism and selfishness often replace the essence of togetherness and sharing.

Instead of imbibing qualities of compassion, generosity, sharing, and caring which the Master has tried to ingrain in us, we are sliding downward to selfishness and individualism, expecting favours in exchange for our donations and demanding VIP status.

Finally, we think that being seen close to the Master qualifies us as VIPs.

Innumerable times the Master has said, "The sangat is my family." As disciples, we are his flock, his family. He has taken our responsibility for us: there is no closer bond than that between a Master and his disciple. The Master has also said that his relatives and friends do not get special treatment or blessings by having closer access. If they did, they would all be enlightened by now.

We often hear him say:

> Do not walk behind me, I cannot lead.
> Do not walk in front of me, I cannot follow.
> Just walk beside me, I need a friend.

It is not a question of one's importance but of listening, following, and working towards our destination together.

It is said: "The Master is like a fire. Stand too close and you'll get burnt; stand too far and you won't get the heat!"

Being "too close" can burn! A "close" disciple may fail to see the Master as a Master. Then the disciple's faith and love go up in flames and burn to ashes.

The opposite extreme – "Stand too far and you won't get the heat" – is not about physical distance. Standing far is when we remove or disassociate ourselves from the tenets of Sant Mat, stray from the teachings, absent ourselves from satsangs, and do not attend to meditation. When we stray so far, we cannot benefit from the teachings nor be receptive to the Master's grace.

In summary:
- Don't try to get too close to the physical Master – you may burn with doubts and lose faith. Remember the saying, "Familiarity breeds contempt."
- Don't run away from the Master – you might not benefit from his presence.
- Just follow the middle path – don't try to be important – just be a humble disciple. Remember, there are no VIPs on this path – just devoted disciples.

Indispensable Sevadars

None of us are indispensable, nor will the Master's work come to a grinding halt because of our absence. When we make a commitment to serve we leave no room for conditions because selfless work is unconditional. A true sevadar has no wants, no demands – only the desire to serve. The true indicator of a satsangi's love for the Master is to do seva without questioning.

There is a haunting saying that speaks volumes of the attitude we should adopt during seva:

> *seva karaange ta mukadi nahi*
> *na karaange ta rukadi nahi.*

> If we want to do seva,
>   it will always be available in abundance;
> but if we do not wish to do it,
>   it will never stop because of that.

Initially our enthusiasm knows no bounds, our earnest desire makes us plead for seva and we ask for any seva, any time, any place and under any condition. But as soon as we are given seva we develop an attitude. Our demands and expectations begin to mount. On the other hand, when we give of ourselves in seva, when we lose our individuality working for humanity, we open ourselves to enduring success.

No seva is important or unimportant; all seva is equal. If we believe that seva is given by the Master, then it has to be important. Just as a car cannot run on three wheels, or a body is not whole if a limb is missing, here too, one seva supports the others. All sevas are intimately linked. Doing seva should be a "high" – a *"nasha"* (intoxication) or *"janoon"* (obsession). We become so engrossed that nothing else matters.

Look at the sevadars in agriculture, horticulture, langar, sanitation, *luk* (road-building) seva – day or night, hot or cold, rain or shine, they carry on their seva relentlessly. They don't complain of the weather, of the lack of fans, coolers, or air-conditioning. They are not looking for cold water to quench their thirst. Neither do they look for comfortable chairs and better accommodations. They are *"mast,"* blissfully happy, completely absorbed and intoxicated with seva – not perched in comfort-able offices getting flustered when the electricity goes off or the phones go on the blink, or ordering tea or coffee to while away the time or just watching the clock and waiting to go home.

Let's keep this in mind: as long as the Master wants us to do his work, he will give us the strength, brains, energy, and health to do it. But we can lose it all in a flash with a stroke, brain haemorrhage, amnesia, Alzheimer's or paralysis. None of us will be spared, none of us will escape. We are nobodies – we need to take the self away and give of the self instead.

We do not have the capacity to do anything on our own. No doubt we start with good intentions but some obstacle comes in the way. It bounces off the ground and into the air, this big ego of ours. We begin to expect a reward, a pat on the back, we want recognition and power. Our ego takes hold of us. We are aware that ego is our worst enemy, yet we cling to it like our life-support system. Seva humbles the inflated ego.

The ocean does not dry up if a drop or wave spills over the shore. Our contribution as individuals is negligible, inconse-quential and insignificant. Individuals can't and don't make the difference. For what can one little drop of water do when faced with the might of the ocean? Strength lies in the wholeness of the ocean and not the individual drop. During seva we are given the opportunity to be a part of the ocean by working together in harmony and joy. Strength lies in the unity, the wholeness of the ocean, not in the uniqueness of an individual drop.

We are mere drops in the ocean. Seva will continue with or without us; none of us are indispensible.

"Extraordinary" Visiting Satsangis

Expectation is the arrogance of the mind – a mind that screams "I," "Me," "Mine." Where there is devotion, there can be no demands or expectations.

Dera was created by the Masters to give us an abode where we can tear ourselves away from the madness in our everyday lives and gain some semblance of serenity within through spiritual practice.

As satsangis, we are expected to imbibe the values of Sant Mat regarding discipline and humility irrespective of who we are, where we live, what status we come from, and what designation we hold. We are expected to conform to Sant Mat values and principles when visiting Dera. Judging others' seva, criticizing the systems and facilities, or flouting the rules and regulations exposes our disrespect and selfishness.

We need to drop our baggage of expectations and ego outside the gates of Dera and walk in as humble devotees, not demanding guests. It is often said: "Whenever someone comes to the divine with full hands, he goes away empty-handed. Whenever someone comes to the divine empty-handed, his hands are filled."

We should come to Dera with empty hands if we want to receive from the divine.

The Master takes every measure to provide a basic level of comfort to his sangat with no bias, despite the limitations arising from the humungous size of the crowds. But we continue to demand more and more. It's a shame that we can be so wrapped up in ourselves, our needs and desires that we forget to be grateful and continue to grumble and complain.

In our self-absorption, we can easily forget the primary reason we visit Dera: to focus on the Master and our discipleship.

Instead we embark on a crusade: the bhojan bhandar is too far; the snack bar queues are too long; the hostel canteens don't have enough variety of food. If there are burgers, why can't there be pizzas? If there are noodles, why not fried rice? We expect a food court at our doorstep. Next we will demand room service with an à la carte menu.

At the satsang pandal, everyone wants to be seated in front. While it is understandable that most of us would like to sit in front to see the Master up close, we often have mixed motives. Many of us suffer from this disease called VIP; we want to be seen in front to enhance our status, our ego. In the Master's court, no one is special; we are all equal.

Despite Dera's best efforts to make accommodations available online, via a first-come-first-serve booking system, we demand a specific hostel or room if we are not satisfied with what we are allotted. Some of us even ignore the request to book in advance and stroll in as "walk-ins" expecting certain rooms. Some even feign medical conditions to justify getting a certain room. If we can book a train or flight to travel here, why can't we pre-book our accommodation? Can we hop on to a train or aircraft without a prior booking?

The Master's schedule is announced one year in advance to give us ample time to plan our visits, so we have no excuse for not booking reservations in advance. We seem to be busier than the Master himself!

When we don't get what we want, we target the sevadars, questioning their attitude and complaining about them. First we need to delve into our own attitude: Did we help the Dera administration by conforming to the simple regulations for the smooth functioning of this colossal organization?

The Masters lovingly built Dera for all of us. Dera belongs to every one of us, everyone is welcome. But just as we expect a certain semblance of consideration from our family members within our own homes, it's the same here. Dera is our home, but we need to be considerate and respect the facilities that have been so painstakingly organized.

Let us leave our demands behind, deflate the ego, drop our expectations, adhere to the regulations, accept the conditions, and relinquish our imagined status. Let's just be disciples, not guests with endless demands.

We are at Dera for a limited time. Instead of trying to change the system for the few days we are here, let's adapt and change ourselves by knocking off the ego that is shackling us.

As we enter the gates of Dera, let's respect the sacredness of this place which the Masters have built with selfless love, devotion, and dedication, and stay within the discipline expected of us.

Let's come with our heads bowed and hands folded as disciplined disciples and humbly absorb what we are here for. Come to the divine empty handed and go with our hands and hearts full.

Dera Sevadars Are Evolved Souls

This is rather ticklish!

Dera sevadars do not attain enlightenment by living in the confines of the colony and neither are they better or superior in any way. They are as ordinary as the rest of us.

The eternal disease which spreads like an epidemic amongst sevadars everywhere is that of self-importance. Everyone is affected. We are consumed with titles and positions, to the point where some want to leave seva if a title is not awarded to them.

Positions are given for administrative purposes, not to inflate the ego. A position may come with some authority, but to do seva by wielding power or pushing people around is destructive. A person with a title or position ultimately makes no difference. It is the team that runs an organization. It is the sevadars down the line that keep the machinery well oiled.

With inflated egos, the essence of seva gets buried. An individual is but a miniscule grain in this enormous set-up. Our presence here is inconsequential; we don't matter, we don't make a difference, we're not indispensable, the seva won't stop because of our absence.

Let's introspect: We sit in comfortable offices with air-conditioning and heaters, forgetful of the plight of those working in the blistering heat or the harsh cold – yet we have the gumption to complain.

We live in spacious houses and don't have a thought about those who sleep on hard floors in the sheds – but still we are dissatisfied.

We are graciously given subsidies, but we always want more – our desires are endless.

We are living in a pollution-free environment, a life incomparable to any other in the world, but we are unappreciative.

We see truckloads of sevadars coming from various places; they do what is required of them and leave as silently as they came. No fuss, no recognition. That is the attitude we need to adopt. We need to be silent, inconspicuous sevadars.

We should strip ourselves of ranks, titles, politics, and the everyday hassles that haunt our daily lives and serve with humility. Here is an ideal situation where ranks and positions don't matter, where promotions and positions are irrelevant, where the only thing that matters is our humanity, devotion, and love, and the obedience to serve unselfishly.

Here and now we can change from being involved to evolved!

In the final analysis – who are we?

As the Bible says: "Dust you are and to dust shall you return."[36]

Dera is the place where the Master wiped out class distinction with one stroke at the langar. That is our true inheritance; that is the richness of character we have to imbibe from the Master.

The Master has set a high benchmark for us and that should be our goal: to be a good human being, to practise equality for all, and serve without expectation, ego, or pride.

Heaven and Hell

A story is sometimes told about the Sufi mystic, Rabia of Basra:

Rabia was running through the marketplace with a burning torch in one hand and a bucket of water in the other.

People asked her, "What are you doing?"

She replied: "I am doing the thing that should have been done long before. I am going to burn this idea of heaven above and drown the idea of hell below. Both are fake; they are not part of geography, they are inside us. It depends on us if we live in hell or heaven."[37]

Heaven and hell are our own creation. We can choose to live in the depths of hell with anger and hate or nurture the values of love and compassion and live in heaven.

Where there is no love and compassion, there is no heaven, no spirituality.

In today's society there is little concern for the elderly. Old age homes are increasing because we have no place in our homes and hearts for our parents. They are left to fend for themselves alone, old, and helpless.

We have no time for our parents who held our little fingers and taught us to walk, who ached with pain when we had a fall, who wept deep inside when we cried, who deprived themselves in order to feed and educate us, and who stayed up all night nursing us when we were ill.

But today when they need us to hold their hand, we have no time. When they need us to care for them, we have no concern. When they need us to love them, our love has run dry. We too will be old one day, and that day is not far off. Just as we cut our parents out of our lives, our children will do the same. The Buddhist saying is apt: "Do good, get good, do bad, get bad!"[38]

Children on the streets are scavenging for food, while we host lavish dinners and don't have a heart big enough to slip our hands in our wallets and buy these starving children some food. Do we participate in social responsibility by educating one child? See the advertisements urging us to pay for just one child's education, the cost of which is so paltry it would embarrass us. It's not sufficient to only *feel* sympathy for the deprived. We should do something!

If we want to live in love, we need to love and respect others, and if we want to serve humanity we need to serve with humility.

Where there is no humility, the effect of seva is nullified.

In seva we go through a learning process, a cleansing process, an awareness process. Seva gives us the opportunity to realize our flaws. Seva is easy for those who want to give, but difficult for those who want to receive. It is a silent offering of our love for the Master. Seva is when we unconsciously begin to discard or disregard the self because we are intensely absorbed only in serving. It is a way to express our devotion, a feeble effort to surrender, so that we may humble our egos.

As Maharaj Sawan Singh Ji said: "Seva has many rewards, but the unique one is that a person imbibes the qualities of the person whom he serves."[39]

Baba Ji repeatedly stresses that we should work collectively, shoulder to shoulder, irrespective of caste, creed, colour and social status. In seva there is no king or pauper, senior or junior, official or labourer. In the Master's ocean of love there is room only for the helpless, humble, surrendering soul.

We can create heaven or hell within us – the choice is ours. What will you choose?

Good and Bad Satsangs

We talk of some satsangs being good and others bad.

But if we agree that all satsangs are based on the teachings, then how can we differentiate a good satsang from a bad one? If the teachings are good, then the satsang is good.

Satsangs are not given for entertainment. This is not a stage for showing off public speaking skills. Satsangs are meant to clarify the teachings and inspire us to practise meditation. We need spiritual discourses to motivate and inspire us. Just one word in a satsang can change our thinking and attitude. Just one line might turn our life around. Even if we absorb one word or one line in a satsang, it has served its purpose. We need to be ready to learn and absorb.

There was a seeker who went to a master and asked for instruction in the truth. The master very simply said:

"Everything is consciousness and thou art that. That is the truth."

"Is that all?" the seeker asked. "Can't you elaborate?"

"That's all I have to teach. If you want something else, you will have to find another master."

Disappointed, the seeker left and eventually found his way to another master who had a large ashram and many disciples.

The seeker asked the new master, "I want to know the truth. Please instruct me."

With a glance, the master understood what kind of seeker he was. "Have you been to another master?"

"Oh yes," said the seeker, "but he couldn't instruct me on the truth."

"All right, I will give you the instruction. But first you will have to serve me for twelve years without question. We need someone to pick up the cow dung. Are you willing to do that?"

"Yes," said the seeker enthusiastically. And he was taken into the ashram. At the end of twelve years, he said to the master, "Twelve years are over. Please instruct me on the truth."

"Very good," said the master, "here is my teaching; everything is consciousness, and thou art that."

Bewildered, the seeker said meekly, "But that is exactly what the other master told me."

"Of course," replied the master, "The truth hasn't changed in twelve years and never will."

"But why did I have to spend twelve years picking up cow dung?" asked the seeker.

The master replied, "Because your mind was too clogged to understand. The master has to say only one word, and the truth will explode within the disciple."[40]

Our minds are clogged! Satsangs clear those blockages.

Satsangs inspire us to move in the direction where the truth will explode within us.

All satsangs carry the same message; they are neither good nor bad. Satsangs are meaningful.

Turning "I Am" into "I Am Not"

We experience years of struggle and pain, but what really is the crux of our pain?

Plato describes a man as a circle which was cut in two halves, and now he runs around trying to be whole again.[41]

If we look around us, there is not a single person who is at peace with himself. Everyone feels there is something lacking in their lives. The rich and poor, the young and old, the sick and healthy – it's the same with everyone. Everyone feels incomplete and dissatisfied. As the saint Sahjo Bai taught, "The rich are unhappy; the poor are the very picture of misery."[42]

We think our happiness lies in satisfying material cravings, but it is the desire to be whole again that causes our restlessness, so possessions can't satisfy us. That desire to feel whole comes from our separation from our origin, our source. The seeking and searching is *birha*, the yearning to meet our creator. Separation from our creator causes our restlessness.

We run around in circles trying to attain that which is transitory, but we shy away from that which is permanent and within our reach. We've tried to achieve happiness through worldly and materialistic things, via family, friends and money. None of those make us feel whole. There is still a void in our lives despite the heights of any success we may have achieved. We've tried and lost – because that something which is missing is permanence and wholeness.

Despite the fact that there are exciting temptations everywhere we look, there is emptiness within. This is because no outward thing or person can give us real joy. Being with the Master, just seeing his physical form and hearing his voice, is more soothing than all the worldly pleasures. If the Master's physical form can draw gigantic crowds and bring people together from all over the world, can we for one moment imagine the exhilaration of seeing his true form?

We need to put our love into action. Just saying "I love the Master" is not enough. "When the heart is full, the lips are sealed," said Sri Ramakrishna Paramahansa.[43]

To truly love the Master is to dissolve the self so that only he exists. "I am" must become "I am not."

Kabir said: "If I am, He is not; and if He is, I am not."[44]

And Guru Nanak said, *"tera, tera, tera"* – meaning "yours, yours, yours."

When Death Knocks

"Although it is uncertain when or how we will die, it is absolutely certain that we will surely die."[45] We may guess, reason, study books, and stretch our imagination but we remain ignorant about death. While death fascinates some, it scares others; while some are obsessed with it, others fear it. And some even deny it. But it grips us all; it's the ultimate eventuality, the only certainty, the end of all motion.

We arrive in this world crying and leave it crying – in between, we live in illusion. Talking about death is considered morbid, and many people believe that even mentioning it is to risk wishing it upon themselves, like a bad omen. Some look upon it with a naive, thoughtless cheerfulness, thinking that for some unknown reason death will work out all right for them.

Both attitudes are an evasion of the truth. Death is neither depressing nor exciting; it is simply a fact of life. Actually the word death is a misnomer, for there is no death; at the end of life we simply take off the coat of flesh and leave this physical world.

Death does not defer to anyone. There is a saying:

> In the democracy of the dead, all men are equal. The poor man is as rich as the richest, and the rich man as poor as the pauper. The creditor loses his usury and the debtor is acquitted of his obligations; there, the proud man surrenders his dignity; the politician his honours, and the worldly his pleasures.

There is nowhere to run or hide when death knocks!

When death strikes, there is no difference between the young or old, the healthy or sick, the rich or poor, a king or a beggar. When the time comes, it comes without warning or respect for anyone, and no circumstances can prevent it. No matter who we are, where we are, how impervious to health or wealth we may be, death spares no one. Eventually, all of us will have a prefix added to our name, "late" so-and-so. Dead, buried, gone forever and forever forgotten!

The only way to overcome death is to "die while living" – through meditation and the spiritual way of life.

We are aware that our brief span of life on this earth is not our real existence. There must be something beyond the physical body that survives the demise of the flesh. While the body yearns to live forever in this human garb, the soul craves to be released, for the soul can truly live only when the body dies, first during meditation – dying while living – and then when we drop our human garb at our physical death.

A disciple persistently asked his Master over and over again: What happens after death? When we die, where do we go?

The Master finally asked for a candle to be brought and lit. When the candle was lit, he blew it out and then asked, "Where has the flame gone?"

The disciple was at a loss.

The Master explained, "Just like this – when we die, we disappear. Where has the candle flame gone? It has become one with the whole. Now it no longer exists as an individual flame, the individuality is dropped."

We become part of the whole. When our flame blows out, when we die, we merge with the truth, the One.

Let's prepare ourselves through spiritual practice, knock off our ego and attachments, and ready ourselves when death comes knocking. Be ready, be prepared!

Faith

What is faith?

There was a robber sitting on the side of the road under the shade of a tree. A priest came along and sat by the roadside *dhaba* (food stall). People quickly arranged a comfortable chair for him and served him tea and snacks. Suddenly people came running towards him in total commotion. The priest asked what the noise was all about. The village head said excitedly, "There is a man from another village claiming that God can go through the eye of a needle."

The priest smiled and said grandly:

"It is nonsense. How can God go through the eye of a needle? This villager is a madman, ignore him."

The crowd started to move away quietly when the robber, sitting under the tree with his hat covering his face, softly said: "God! He can do anything!"

That is faith!

The priest, despite all his learning and wisdom, did not have the ultimate faith that God has unlimited powers, while the robber, despite his life and crimes, recognized the power of God. It is said: "Sometimes a sinner wins where a saint misses."

Faith is a belief in things that our senses have not experienced and our mind does not understand. Faith is in believing what we cannot prove. Faith supplies staying power. We can keep going when the going is good, but something extra is needed to keep us balanced when it seems that everything is against us – faith sustains us. By the power of faith, every enduring work is accomplished.

If faith varies with the differing conditions in our lives, it is not faith. Even our marriage vows declare in sickness or in health, for better or for worse – this should apply to our faith too, no matter what adversity we face in our lives.

God sows miracles by handfuls around us:

Isn't every hour of the light and dark a miracle?

Isn't it a miracle that the face of every human being is different?

Isn't it a miracle that a child born to any nationality, anywhere in the world, any caste, creed or colour utters the same first word – Mama?

Isn't it a miracle to see the colours of the rainbow?

Science and technology cannot match any one of these miracles. Science may take man to the moon; but it cannot create another moon. It cannot create another sun. It may achieve the cloning of animals but not the creation of an original. Miracles only work through our faith. Where there is no faith, there can be no miracle; where there is faith, we can see miracles in everything around us. "Faith and Truth are the same thing – on God's side is Truth; on our side is Faith."[46]

A perfect example is the story of Saint Nizamuddin Aulia, who had twenty-two disciples, each of whom wished to be appointed as his successor. To determine which of them was the most sincere and devoted, Nizamuddin decided to test them.

Walking the streets in the marketplace one day, they strolled into an area of brothels. To the amazement of all those watching, the Master entered one of the brothels, asking all the disciples to stay behind. They stood shocked wondering what the Master was doing in this place.

Nizamuddin asked the woman if she could spare him a room for the night and also to send him some cooked vegetables and sherbet to drink.

The disciples watching from outside could see food and drinks being carried into his room. Imagining the worst, they were filled with despair. How could the Master betray their trust by indulging in food, wine and women? As the night wore on, one by one they slowly began to leave in disgust. Only one of them was waiting when the Master came down the next morning.

When asked why he too did not leave along with the others, he said,

"Master, my only abode is at your feet."

Only one disciple had faith in the Master, only he believed in his Master totally. It was Amir Khusro, whose love was echoed in his poetry for Nizamuddin Aulia, and we remember him through that poetry till today.[47]

Do we have faith or not?

We take our doubts to exaggerated heights and let them grow out of proportion. Situations are not necessarily as they seem. As disciples we will face situations which are mere illusions but seem real at that time.

We will encounter difficulties, frustrations, contradictions, and imperfections because our mind is not spiritually stable. If we succumb to these obstacles, they will blind us to the essential and enduring value of the teachings. Our impatience will drag us away from our commitment to the truth.

We come on the path with enthusiasm and hope, yet lose heart when the smallest unavoidable obstacle arises. This is because we lack faith. Unless we free ourselves from our ignorance, these obstacles will jeopardize our commitment and perspective. If love, trust, determination, and resilience are our foundation, then faith is not far behind.

Head or Tails

When the mind finds a simple solution, like two and a half hours of daily meditation, it cannot grasp it. Because how could anything be so simple? There has to be more, something perhaps we haven't been told! We would probably be more satisfied if we were told to stand on our head for three hours, or stick our heads in the sand like an ostrich to attain liberation. That would satisfy our mind. Perhaps then we could justify not being able to do it.

We spend time aimlessly puttering around, doing everything but the one thing that matters. How many times have we been asked, "What are you doing?" and prompt comes the answer: "Nothing much!" Well, let's put something into that nothing, a little bit of substance, a little bit of meditation. We might be having a perfectly normal day, but when it comes to meditation, we are suddenly too tired, exhausted, depressed, or even too deliriously happy to sit. We conveniently develop a toothache, headache, or a backache. Our excuses are infinite!

"Time and tide waits for no man." If we've lost a day of meditation, we cannot make up for it – the moment has passed. And we get even further from our goal than we were yesterday.

When will we find time for meditation? When we are on our deathbed? When a personal tragedy strikes? Too late, wouldn't you say? The time once lost will not come back.

There is no running away now, except to run within. Our desire has to be deep and desperate, for only if we have tremendous hunger and thirst for truth can we find it. We have to walk the path of tears, tears of inexplicable agony of longing and separation. There are no half-measures in spirituality, it's everything or nothing!

It's a do or die situation.

So the Master pushes us to give it our all, give up everything. Do or die; die while living. Just let go – dare to let go – dare to die! Because meditation is a preparation for death. Meditation defies death because we learn to die while living – so the Master pushes us to dare death by dying daily!

Mullah Nasruddin didn't go to his work one day. In the evening he told his friend he was very happy because he had slept all day. He was asked if he had taken leave from work.

He replied, "No, but I tossed a coin in the morning to see whether to go to work or not. If it showed head down, I'd have to go to work, and if it was tails down, I could take the day off."

"So it came tails down?" he was asked.

"Yes," he replied, "but I had to toss it ten times before it came to tails."[48]

That is our situation with meditation. We toss the coin several times, we toss in bed when the alarm goes off, we toss our mind bargaining for a few minutes more of sleep, perhaps just another five minutes, then we toss and go back to sleep promising ourselves that tomorrow we will start with renewed energy. The next day it's the same, and the same the day after that. And one day, tomorrow doesn't come. It's too late.

If we give in to our laziness and lack of willpower, we could lose our chance forever, for who knows if tomorrow will ever come. Although the desire to seek God-realization is strong, we fall prey to the mind.

None of us would be seekers on the path to liberation if we did not have the desire, but desire alone won't get us results. The desire has to be put into action through our efforts.

Let's be done with tossing a coin and leaving our spiritual birthright to chance. There is no more time for head or tails, no more time for bargaining. Our time is up!

Karma Baggage

What Is Karma?

First and foremost, let's understand that the karma theory is way beyond our understanding. The law of karma is unfathomable and complex. The deeper we delve into it, the more complicated it gets. We can beat our head against the wall, analyze, question, debate, read innumerable texts on it, try to dissect the various types of karmas – *pralabdh* (karma that will bear fruit in this life), *sinchit* (stored or accumulated) and *kriyaman* (karma we produce in this life). We can discuss the difference between the *bhog junis* (the species that are only paying off karma, not creating it) and the *karma junis* (human beings: the species that both pays off and creates karma), but this will serve no purpose because we can never understand karma in its entirety.

The more questions we have, the bigger the confusion. No one has returned from death to give us the actual truth of the complexities of life and death; it will always remain a mystery. Karma theory is endless, like a bottomless sea, and the mind cannot grasp its true reality because our intellect is limited, while the cosmic law is infinite. We are aware that karma is the consequence of our thoughts, words and actions, and that is what we will have to live with.

So before we embark on this tedious journey of asking questions to which there are no satisfying answers, let's just accept that karma theory – the principle of "as you sow, so shall you reap" – exists beyond any measure of doubt. The Bible puts it this way: "For all things a man shall sow, those also he shall reap."[49]

We need to condition the mind to accept that everything happening to us is because of our karmas. The people we meet and interact with, the skirmishes we have, the person who gives joy and the one who receives it, the one who inflicts hurt and the one who is hurt, birth and death, all and everything – accepting that our existence is determined by our karmas makes it easier to deal with it all. By delving any deeper, we will rake up never ending questions, which will only add to our confusion.

Why rattle our mind with issues that we cannot comprehend? The more sensible approach would be to accept it and deal with it. We can eat a well-cooked meal and enjoy the flavours without getting into the specific ingredients. We can have a pleasurable flight on an aircraft or bask in the sun on a luxury yacht without being bothered about the mechanics involved.

An architect who had worked for a large corporation for many years was given plans for a model house to be constructed. He was told that no expense was to be spared and that he should use the finest materials and craftsmen. During the construction of the house, the architect thought the project was too extravagant. He decided to reap more profits and build the house with inferior materials. After the house was constructed, the chairman of the corporation gave him the keys to the house, saying that the house was a surprise gift for him in gratitude for all his years of hard work in the company.

The architect built a disaster for someone else to live in but received the results of his actions instead. This is karma.

J. P. Vaswani has said:

We have tried to understand that everything that comes to man is of his own doing. In other words, man is the builder of his own destiny.... What you send comes back to you. The law of karma is thus the law of the boomerang. It is an inviolable law that governs the universe from end to end."[50]

We attain human life by gradually transmigrating from the various species of plants, birds, and animals to the top of the creation. Human beings are considered the top of the creation because we can discriminate between right and wrong. Each thought, word and action creates karma – right thoughts, words and actions manifest into positive karmas, and harmful thoughts, words and actions into negative karmas. Eventually every human being has to submit to the bondage of the karmas he or she has created through each individual action.

Our karmas have tarnished our true self.

Take the example of a kettle that has never been cleaned; the layers of dirt grow over it and make it appear black. When the kettle is thoroughly cleaned – scrubbed, rinsed, and polished – its true quality, brightness and lustre shine again. Its beauty was there all along; it was simply hidden, concealed.

It's the same with us – once we have cleansed ourselves of desires, cravings, and thoughts, our divinity will shine through. Our divinity was always part of us, but it was buried, covered with layers of cravings and negative thoughts. Spiritual attainment means adapting to higher aspirations and thought. It is a way of uncovering the soul, which has been hidden beneath various garbs.

With each cycle of birth and death, the soul continues to evolve, and through spiritual practice, the soul clears the karmas till it finally reaches divine attainment and merges with its source.

Evolution of the Soul

As explained in the Hindu scriptures, we are reincarnated in 8,400,000 life forms, continuously evolving through the plant, insect, bird, and animal kingdoms before we are given a human birth.

We evolve by transmigrating from plants, insects, fish, birds, and mammals, all the way to the "top of the creation" – human beings. The lower species do not generate karmas as they are not endowed with the power of discrimination and remain instinctual by nature. The plants and trees know only sap, sunlight, and moisture through which they survive. Animals are conscious mostly of hunger and thirst; their lives revolve around their strong survival instinct for food and water. They are not endowed with awareness of much else. They are simply paying off karmas.

Human beings on the other hand stand supreme amongst all living creatures by virtue of our superior sense of discrimination. We can use our multifaceted minds to distinguish between right and wrong. Most important, we are given the ability to work our way back to the Creator through the technique of meditation. With the aid of the powerful mind, we can climb to great heights of spiritual attainment or fall prey to temptations and desire.

As humans, we continue to evolve in every birth, from lower consciousness to higher consciousness, until we attain God-realization. The evolution of the soul can take many cycles of birth and death, depending on the weight of karmas. These karmas make up the endless chain of cause and effect, and desire is what sets it motion.

Annamalai Swami says: "All desires can cause you trouble, even spiritual ones."[51]

Unless our karmic debts are paid, the soul will continually be transported back into the cycle of birth and death. The soul's evolution continues even in the human birth. That evolution consists of transforming ourselves and eliminating karma by cultivating a divine connection through an enlightened guide who teaches the art of meditation. The practice of meditation purifies our soul, leading it back to the original spiritual nature, which is the core of our true being.

If we continue to fuel the fire, it will keep burning; if we continue to fuel our karmas, we will keep returning, because karma determines our cyclic existence.

Free Will, Destiny, and Karma

Our rebirth is the consequence of our karmas and impressions from our previous births – our cravings, desires, thoughts and actions. Destiny is the consequence of those karmas. Destiny places us in circumstances where karmas, both negative and positive, can be set into motion.

Our parents, siblings, spouses, colleagues and dealings with others are directly related to our karmas, while destiny arranges those relationships and circumstances so that we can pay off the karmas. At what point we are paying off old karmas or creating new ones is impossible for us to comprehend – that question is an aspect of the universal will that is not revealed to us.

Karma is a law of nature – life is easier when we accept it. Accepting the theory of cause and effect is how we can submit to the law of nature. We simply need to accept that our karma determines what we deserve and what we have to face.

Let's take a situation where karma demands that we have to fracture a leg – look at the role of free will and destiny in that situation:

Free Will: Whether we choose to put the right leg forward or left, walk out through the front door or rear – that is free will. Free will is very limited, almost inconsequential. We have the free will to adopt a negative or positive attitude, to cry or laugh, to be happy or sad. Those are merely emotions and attitudes. Emotions and attitudes can change from one hour to the next, but they cannot change life situations or circumstances. We may believe that our acceptance or rejection of a situation will change the course of our lives, but that is wrong thinking. We will head towards a situation as destiny wills, no matter what our attitude or emotion. However, the attitude that we adopt can help us deal with the situation with either depression or equanimity. Whether we laugh or cry will either lighten or worsen the moment.

Destiny: Destiny creates the circumstances for the karma to manifest. We may use free will to walk out the rear door instead of the front and stick the right leg forward instead of the left. Whether we adopt a positive or negative attitude will not deter destiny from doing its job. Destiny will assert its authority and put us in a situation that will cause us to slip and fall, no matter which choice we exercised. That was our destiny. That situation was predestined; it remains unchanged.

Karma: The fall results in breaking the leg because that was the inevitable karma. Destiny will put us in the situation for that particular karma to be paid off. It was inevitable, bound to happen, and there is no running away from it because that is the karma or debt that was required to be paid. Fracturing the leg was the end result of the karma. Linked to this karma are those people we have to give to or take from. For example, we have karma with the doctor, nurse, chemist, the other people helping us, etc. It's a ripple effect with those connected to our karma. We will go through the physical and emotional trauma as per our individual karma, but at the same time the karmas linked with all these people will also be cleared.

So destiny wills us to move into a situation no matter what preventive measures we take using our so-called free will, and eventually the karma of breaking our leg will take place because that is the final reckoning, the justice for our past deeds. There is no hiding from it or escaping it. Karma is already determined, it will take its course – the debt cannot be left unpaid, nor can it be sold or bargained away.

A Tibetan Buddhist Master taught: "The karma living beings gather is never worn away even after a thousand *kalpas* (aeons). When the time comes and the appropriate conditions gather, the fruit of action will come to maturity."[52]

The law of karma will continue irrespective of who we are – rich or poor, young or old, sinner or priest; whether we protest or submit, argue or believe.

Yes! Masters Have Karmas

Being born again, not of corruptible seed, but of incorruptible, by the word of God, which lives and abides for ever.

For all flesh is as grass, and all the glory of man as the
flower of grass.

The grass withers, and the flower thereof falls away:

But the word of the Lord endures forever.

And this is the word which by the gospel is preached
unto you.

Bible, 1 Peter 1:23

When the Masters are here in the human form – they are born
of the flesh, born with a mind – they take on karmas in order
to live in the body. They have relationships like us – they are
sons and daughters, brothers and sisters, wives and husbands,
mothers and fathers. Since the Masters come here in the
human form, they are susceptible to the vagaries of old age,
prone to illness and certain to die. The previous Masters have
shown this by example; they came in the human form and
honoured their relationships on the human level and then left
the physical plane.

Nevertheless, there is a huge difference between a Master
and us. The Master leads an ordinary life but with extraordinary
qualities. Masters are realized souls connected to their higher
consciousness, so on the spiritual level the Masters are beyond
the realms of sorrow and pain, of attachments, of worldly
senses and desires. They remain untouched by and detached
from human attributes.

Their primary work is to initiate their flock and show them the way to connect to their inner consciousness. Eventually they will leave the physical form – their presence in the human form is merely to connect with us. Their purpose is one-pointed, to attach souls to the absolute truth within.

The unique quality of pristine purity in the Master fills us with joy when we are in his presence – we sense his powerful, energetic, positive vibrations in every cell and nerve of our body. His inner light shines through and totally engulfs us because Masters are born of "the incorruptible seed." That is the example they give us to follow.

The human body is perishable, subject to change, decay and impermanence. This is what it means to be born in "corruptible seed." But to see the kingdom of God, we need to be reborn of the "incorruptible," that which is permanent, unchangeable and indestructible. To be born of the "incorruptible" is to be reborn "by the word of God," which means being born of the spirit – not of the flesh, not of the human body.

Through initiation we are reborn of the spirit. Through initiation and meditation the Master connects us to the Sound Current, the Shabd or Logos, which "lives and abides forever." The creation is sustained by the Shabd, and once we are connected to this Shabd or Sound Current through initiation, our spirit also lives forever.

The Shabd "lives and abides forever" in the Master, as he is born of incorruptible seed – he is one with the Shabd, without attachments. He takes on karmas in order to take life in the body, but he is not subject to those karmas – he is in control.

No! Masters Do Not Erase Karmas

Baba Ji emphatically declares that no power on this earth can take away our karmas – we have to go through them ourselves.

If a son commits a crime, would the father be sentenced and imprisoned instead of the son? No matter how dearly the father loves his son and goes through intense agony because of the son's condition; no matter how deeply he feels his son's desperation and helplessness, tries to protect him, and even arranges for a lawyer, ultimately the son has to go through the sentence himself. Both have their individual karmas which are intrinsically linked – the son goes through the rigours of the punishment, while the father suffers mental anguish. Both go through karmas in different ways – but each has his own debt to pay.

From the time we are born, we know we will die – that is the only reality we know, it's the only certainty. The interim period is an illusion where we go through the dictates of the law of nature, of cause and effect. There is little or no contribution from us in these situations. We are reborn to pay off both good and bad karmas during this time. Our environment, social and financial status, and health are determined according to our karmas.

There may be five siblings in a family, but each is governed by his or her individual karmas. They have the same parents, same upbringing, same education, are exposed to similar situations, yet they are so different from one another, because karmas determine each one's life.

Compare these five siblings to five fingers on one hand. They are in the same family, but they are not the same. One sibling may be a doctor, the other a politician, another a criminal, one a struggling artist, while one turns out a total idler. All five are different from one another despite being exposed to the same upbringing and conditions, because karmas are based on each individual's actions. It's the law of nature, the universal law – karmas cannot be exchanged, planted on another, bargained, sold, or escaped – each individual has to burn his own karmas himself. Our lives are dictated by the law of karma.

The Master does not eliminate our karmas, but he reveals a way to purify the mind, which in turn allows us to divest ourselves of our karmas. The Master does not clear them miraculously. Instead he shows us a method to prepare our mind that helps us accept our fate, keep a positive attitude, and stay balanced while going through our karmas.

The Master's work is not to eliminate karmas but to awaken and purify the mind to overcome their influence.

No Guarantees!

No! There are no guarantees. The so-called guarantee of four human lives and not having to return to the animal kingdom can expire. The law of karma is clear:

> Who sows must reap...and cause must bring the sure effect; good, good; bad, bad; and none escape the law.[53]

This is the irreversible law of karma.

In every sphere of life – in villages, cities, countries, schools, colleges, work places, and so forth – there are laws governing us with a code of conduct, principles, values, rules, and regulations. The world would be totally chaotic if there were no laws. Visas are required to visit foreign countries; there are marriage laws, road regulations, and judicial systems. The entire world functions on systems; if these systems didn't exist, everything would crumble into chaos.

Even in our individual homes we expect a certain semblance of discipline – respecting elders, educating children, working for a living, timings for sleep and meals. Take the human body for instance; we cannot put both legs forward when we walk, we can't see with our eyes closed, we can't eat with our ears or hear with our nose. Each organ has a function. If the digestive system collapses, the body stops functioning; if any of the organs fails, the body goes through a trauma. And all of this is a microcosm of our world, which is guided and constantly governed by rules and regulations, codes of conduct, and laws at every stage.

Let's take the example of driving. When driving, we are compelled to adhere to the traffic regulations. If we break the traffic rules, our license is withdrawn. In every aspect of life, we need to conform to rules – if we break those rules, we will have to reap the consequences. Since all actions have consequences, our future births will be affected. If our actions are low enough, our human lives can be withdrawn.

There are no guarantees.

Guarantees expire when there is an overdose of negative actions. We are then withdrawn from human birth and sent toppling down to the animal kingdom.

Getting a license to drive is akin to being initiated: it's the first step but not the end. Being initiated, adhering to the principles of the teachings, and meditating are different from one another (though of course interrelated). If we break the laws of nature – if we don't obey the teachings – we are liable to pay a heavy penalty. There is no guarantee of four human births or of being born as a human being again after we are initiated. Being initiated is only the beginning, the means, but practising daily meditation is the end.

Purification through meditation is the only guarantee of receiving the precious garb of the human body and saving ourselves from the horrors of birth in lower kingdoms.

In our everyday lives, we protect ourselves by saving for a rainy day, by investing in health insurance, by eating nourishing food. It is the same in the spiritual world. We can protect ourselves from rebirth or being thrown back to the animal kingdom through the powerful practice of meditation.

Mind and Madness

God's Greatest Creation

The most outstanding wonder of God's creation is the human mind. The mind is at the same time strong yet weak, sincere yet deceitful; it can take man to the heights of success and to the depths of destruction. It is the most intriguing, mysterious and yet the most disastrous and deadly of man's possessions.

There is no other machinery that is so complex, yet so subtle, and with such infinite possibility. The way we use this instrument called mind is completely up to us. We can destroy with it or utilize it positively to its maximum potential. Such is the power of the mind!

We indulge our mind because of our weakness and lack of self-control, giving the mind ruthless power. We make ourselves slaves to our mind by giving it total freedom, letting it run wild and loose. We should be the navigators of our mind, but instead we let our mind steer us whichever way it wants. And who can deny that the mind is most of the time stupid, and only sometimes wise. We talk of free will, reason, logic, intellect, understanding – but our words, thoughts, and actions demonstrate that we rarely exercise any of those faculties.

Mirdad says: "Think as if your every thought were to be etched in fire upon the sky for all and everything to see. For so, in truth, it is."[54]

Think deeply about this. We would probably not even be able to live with ourselves if we admitted to ourselves the thoughts we have. We would be appalled at ourselves if we were to expose the thoughts that constantly stream through our minds. We might be rudely shocked to discover the filth and anger we have accumulated in our mind over the years.

Here is a poignant description: "Our minds are like crows. They pick up everything that glitters, no matter how uncomfortable our nests get with all that metal in them."[55]

And all that unnecessary glittering metal in our mind has festered into five deadly diseases which shackle the mind. Every thought, word or action can either enhance the mind so it can focus better or steer it away from its original source. The Masters emphasize the necessity to control and overcome the five passions through meditation – *kam* (lust), *krodh* (anger), *lobh* (greed), *moh* (attachment), and *ahankar* (ego). They are the major obstacles and hindrances to spiritual progress.

These passions need to be harnessed and tamed. As Mahatma Gandhi said, once our senses are out of control, it's like "sailing in a rudderless ship, bound to break into pieces when it comes in contact with the very first rock."[56]

An old man describes an experience going on in his mind to his grandson:

"There's a terrible fight between two wolves going on in us all. One is evil – he is anger, envy, sorrow, regret, greed, arrogance, self-pity, guilt, resentment, inferiority, lies, false pride, superiority, and ego. The other is good – he is joy, peace, love, hope, serenity, humility, kindness, benevolence, empathy, generosity, truth, compassion, and faith. This same fight is going on inside you and inside every other person too."

The grandson thought about it and asked his grandfather, "Which wolf will win?"

The old man simply replied, "The one you feed."[57]

The wolf we feed will determine if the good within us has triumphed.

Destructive Lust – *Kam*

There is a story of a sage who had been in meditation for many years and was considered a great soul by his disciples and peers. After having spent many years in caves and forests in solitude and meditation, he was returning to his village. On reaching a river, he asked a fisherman to take him across. The fisherman was busy, so his daughter offered to ferry the sage across.

During the boat ride, the sage started feeling attracted to the fisherman's daughter. He kept eyeing her and eventually his lust overcame him. Just one moment of weakness dragged the sage down to the depths of destruction. By losing control of his mind, he lost the spiritual progress he had gained through his years of solitude and intense meditation. He was back where he started, all because he could not bring his lustful mind under control.

We need to dominate the mind instead of letting the mind overpower us. When a ship is drifting, an anchor is used to hold it down. Likewise when our mind is wandering, only constant simran can hold the mind steady. Simran works like a shock absorber, protecting and containing the mind's onslaughts. Through simran we can steer the mind back into focus.

The Buddha said: "If the light is on in a house, thieves avoid it; and if the watchman is awake, thieves will not even try."[58]

The house is our mind. The light is the simran. The thieves are negative thoughts.

Keep the light on in the house, keep the simran flowing continuously. Then the thieves – temptations and negative thoughts – won't enter the house of the mind. The light of simran will prevent the thieves, our negative thoughts, from gaining entry.

At initiation, we are told to keep the simran flowing 24/7, to let it flow as naturally as our breathing, without thought or effort, till it seeps into our system so deeply that we are not even conscious of it.

Waking or sleeping, simran should remain with us, working as the mind's watchman, shielding and protecting our house and not allowing the thief of negativity to enter.

The Retarding Effect of Anger — *Krodh*

The dangerous result of indulging in anger is expressed forcefully in the Talmud:

"Anger deprives a sage of his wisdom, and a prophet of his vision."[59]

Anger makes us blind, erratic, impulsive, and rash. There is no passion that shakes the clarity of our judgment and balance as much as anger. It is said that "anger is a wind that blows out the lamp of the mind."[60]

When caught in the midst of anger, we expose our true self. We tend to use anger to hide our insecurity and incompetence. It corrodes our mental state. Even though our pain and hurt are often what causes our anger, we are still responsible for its effects.

A disciple said to his Master, "I have a terrible temper."

The Master said, "Show me your temper."

The disciple replied, "But I don't have it right now."

The Master said, "Then bring it to me when you have it."

The disciple replied, "I can't do that. It just happens suddenly, and by the time I get it to you, I will surely lose it."[61]

Time is the key word here. Time heals and eases every emotion. Time lowers the intensity of an emotion and dissolves the temper.

The moment we become aware of our anger, the emotion begins to dissipate and the intensity drops. Time changes the focus, the energy and the mood. From a negative feeling we can slowly move to a space of equanimity.

Awareness makes us stop and think, it calms us, it forces us to see reason, so by the time we try to vent our temper on someone, it has begun to dissolve.

When we hurt or humiliate someone in anger, we have to deal with the negativity ourselves. The other person can walk away without letting our anger affect him. But we are the ones who must suffer the consequences.

First negativity grabs hold of us, then we lose our temper, then we react, then we remain in a grouchy mood, then we are embarrassed, then we want to hide and run away from people because of the embarrassment and, most important, it nags our conscience. It deprives us of sleep and makes us mentally uncomfortable. The wound festers within us; we can't run away from it.

We have to heal the wound, heal the anger by becoming aware of it – not by denying it. By watching our mind and being aware of our anger, we can slowly change it.

Cancerous Greed – *Lobh*

The early Christian author Tertullian expresses the thought beautifully: "Nothing that is God's is obtainable by money."[62]

No dispute there! We constantly hear about outrageous scams. See how the mighty fall, exposed by scams! Fathers and sons take each other to court and the relationship that was nurtured over many years is lost between the lawyers and the courts. We sell our souls; we lose our integrity, honour, and conscience because of greed.

Very few can escape the lure of glamour, fame, money, and power. We are all victims of the same disease, some to a lesser and others to a greater degree. Our greed overrides our reason.

Money determines who our friends will be, who we will recognize as family and, worst of all, who we will be.

It is said: "A man with one watch knows what time it is. A man with two watches is never quite sure."

Take a look at those who have custom-made mattresses and feather pillows, watch soap operas and pop sleeping tablets to lull themselves to sleep, listen to music to soothe their soul, yet toss and turn all night. The mind is always on the prowl for more and more. We are constantly dissatisfied. Moreover, greed infiltrates the mind and makes it unscrupulous, causing us to cut corners and cheat when we think we won't get caught.

And now take the example of the poor: they sleep on the hard floor with no cloth to cover them. Their day's meal is probably just a slice of bread. They lie on the pavement amidst the noise and dust, yet they sleep soundly.

The accumulation from greed is short-lived. We can learn from Alexander the Great, who went out to conquer and plunder the world, amassed wealth, and never tired of accumulating more and more. According to legend, in his last days he said: "When I die, keep my hands out of the coffin for the world to see that we take nothing with us. We come empty-handed and leave empty-handed."

This truth is beautifully described in a proverb: "When you realize there is nothing lacking, the whole world belongs to you."

When nothing is lacking, then everything is ours and nothing is ours.

Then there is nothing to possess and nothing to lose.

When we don't feel the lack of anything, we become desireless.

In this state, when greed dissolves, "the whole world belongs to you"!

Fatal Bondage of Attachment – *Moh*

The hypnotic power of attachment of any kind clings to our mind as a leech clings to human flesh. The moment we are attached to something is the exact moment we become a slave to it. That attachment causes imbalance in our life.

It has been said that there are two occasions on which the Lord smiles. First when the doctor comes to the bedside of a child who is seriously ill and is about to die, and says to his mother, "Why madam, there is no cause for anxiety; I take upon myself the responsibility of saving your son's life."

Next the Lord smiles when two brothers, who are busy partitioning their land, take a measuring tape, put it across the land and say, "This side is mine, that side is yours."[63]

Yours and mine! And God laughs!

One masterstroke from him and nothing is ours. With one sweep God can bring everything in our lives to a grinding halt. Children, parents, spouses, wealth, property – nothing belongs to us, nothing lasts. Attachments are illusions. When the final moment comes, when death knocks on the door, no relationship, no material possession accompanies us. We leave alone and empty-handed.

All that we have so laboriously and proudly collected and achieved in our lifetime – the titles attached to our names, the nameplates outside our homes, business companies bearing our name, sons to carry on the family name – all are erased and washed away. Death is proof of the waste of attachment. Nothing belongs to us in this transitory world. Everything and everyone perishes.

As the nineteenth-century poet William Winter wrote:

Ambition has but one reward for all: a little power, a little transient fame, a grave to rest in and a fading name.[64]

Power, name and fame eventually wilt away in the grave. And who remembers us after we are buried? How many days does one cry for a dear one who has died? These attachments are illusory.

Only one attachment is imperishable and immortal – our attachment to the truth. This can be achieved only if we rid our mind of the falseness, glitter and superficiality of this world and attach it to meditation. It is said: "If there is a small hole at the bottom of a jar of water, all the water will leak out."[65]

Similarly, if there is the smallest tinge of attachment in us, our attention will be drawn out. Our focus will wane. Instead of heading straight, we will go backwards. Attachments will hold us back from our course.

Every human mind is two-fold: pure when it is free from attachments and impure when it is governed by attachments.

Ego — *Ahankar*

Sri Ramakrishna Paramahansa explains the soaring power of ego in these words:

> The ego of a common man is easier to fade away
> Than the ego of a sage,
> which is hard indeed to wear away.[66]

The ego is like an empty glass that dips itself into the ocean and after filling itself to the brim cries out: "This is me."

But who are we? "Dust you are and to dust shall you return."[67] If we can understand the depth of these words, we will realize that our swollen concern for ourselves, our arrogance and our self-importance, constitutes the worst threat in life.

Take the example of kings, prime ministers, and presidents — their arrogance makes them believe that people are saluting them rather than their position. Receiving adoration should be a humbling experience, instead it makes these so-called rulers dizzy with power and their ego soars.

The positions these people hold may remain, but the people themselves constantly change.

Here is an example from the life of Napoleon Bonaparte:

Napoleon was defeated at war and taken to the island of Saint Helena. One evening while going for a walk, an old lady was passing by from the opposite direction with a load of grass on her back. She was told to step aside because the mighty Napoleon Bonaparte was passing by. Not aware of who he was, she demanded, "Let him step aside, can't he see I'm an old woman carrying such a big load?" Napoleon moved aside to let her pass and said to the guard accompanying him, "The time when mountains used to give way to Napoleon is gone; the soap bubble is no longer there. Now I have to give way to women carrying grass."[68]

He was now a nonentity. His ego had taken a beating. The mighty Napoleon had fallen!

Presidents, prime ministers, senior officials, and chairmen enjoy their short-lived glory and then quietly fade into oblivion, forgotten.

Even a fool can become a hero at some time or another. Great occasions can rouse even the lowest human being to some kind of greatness. Our ego is fed by the mind. It is an illusion caused by our ignorance – "like the glow-worm who after dusk thinks he is giving light to the world. But when the stars begin to twinkle, the light of the glow-worm is humbled."[69]

Only if our mind is empty of self will it be able to receive. In the empty mind there are many possibilities, in the egoistic mind there are few. We will be happiest when our ego has been reduced to zero.

Swami Paramananda has said, "It is the ego that is the great bar to spiritual progress. If you want ego, then you can't have God. If you want God, then you must be crowned with humility."[70]

Awaken to Better Understanding

The Master constantly and persistently urges us to meditate. Time and again, in books, talks and discourses, quotations and analogies, we are warned that the mind is a very powerful instrument that needs to be channelized towards positivity and purity.

Swami Vivekananda said: "The greatest conqueror of the world finds himself a mere child when he tries to control his own mind. This is the world he has to conquer – the greater and more difficult world to conquer."[71]

Saints and sages deliberately give examples which shake us from our slumber, give us a jolt, make us sit up and think deep and hard. If even seers, who have attained a certain level of spiritual progress, are so prone to human frailties, where does it leave us? We have not even begun to climb the first rung of spirituality; our lack of progress leaves us totally vulnerable because we are not able to shield ourselves with meditation. Imagine how susceptible we are, how dangerous our mind is!

There is a saying: "A Master is not just a teacher. A Master is a fire we have to go through, so all that is not gold in us is burnt, and only the pure gold comes out."[72]

The journey on a spiritual path is about going through a cleansing process, a major grinding, a make-over, so to say: it's rough and it's tough. The Master's purpose is to take his disciples back home by removing the impurities and turning us to gold. We need to tame our mind and draw it inwards with meditation to burn and cleanse the impurities.

Sri Ramakrishna Paramahansa has said: "As it is very difficult to gather mustard seeds that escape out of a torn package and get scattered in all directions, so when the human mind runs in diverse directions and is occupied with many things in the world, it is not a very easy task to collect and concentrate it."[73]

This mind runs after worldly things causing it to scatter in all directions. To gather our scattered attention we are given five names to repeat.

The Master says, "There are no failures in Sant Mat."[74]

That makes us winners. Now *that* is a positive thought!

The Master knows we can do it, so we can. Let's set the goal and achieve it. We will win, no matter how tough the journey. Burn those impurities and let the gold shine through. If we tame and harness the mind to focus in the right direction, we will achieve everything!

Shed the Obstacles

Fear of Death

Rumi has said: "Your fear of death is really fear of yourself; see what it is from which you are fleeing."[75]

We fear death because it is unfamiliar. We go to a funeral and see people mourning; the process of grieving for the dead is the process of adjusting to our own shock. We constantly express our intense desire for the eternal truth, yet we live in fear of the very same desire.

Each breath we take is a breath closer to death. Every week, month, year that passes should remind us that death is knocking on our door. We joyfully celebrate birthdays, but each birthday brings us closer to death, so in actual fact we should be celebrating death. We have placed our trust in a life which is sustained by so uncertain a thing as breathing in and out. Yet each breath may be our last.

We are not afraid at the prospect of losing consciousness when we are asleep; we accept sleep as a state of freedom, welcome it as a form of relaxation and look forward to it as a peaceful rest. So it should be with death. If we could experience or know death while living, then surely all fear would cease. The mystery can be unveiled; the unknown can be made familiar; so there need not be fear. When we talk of death, most of us act like children in the dark. To dispel their fear, children turn on the light. To dispel the fear of death, we can turn to the light within. "If thine eye be single, thy whole body shall be full of light."[76]

When we are in constant simran with focussed concentration at the eye centre, that is when our "eye is single"; our inner spiritual "eye" sees within, and the inner light floods our being. This light gives us inner wisdom – "thy whole body shall be full of light." That light, that inner wisdom, dispels our fears and gives us unshakeable faith.

There is a parable of a Japanese samurai warrior and his wife who were crossing over to an island on a small boat.

Suddenly a fierce storm rocked their little boat, and they were in danger of the boat capsizing, and they would drown. The wife was terrified. She started trembling and crying, pleading with her husband to save them. He just sat there motionless.

Nervously she called out to him: "Are you just going to let us drown? Won't you do something?"

The samurai silently pulled his sword from its sheath and held it menacingly against her throat.

Seeing this, she started laughing.

"Why are you laughing? he asked. "This sword is razor-sharp. Just one movement and your throat will be slit."

To which she confidently replied, "The sword might be dangerous, but it is in your hands. And that is enough for me. I trust you completely, that's why I'm not afraid."

The samurai put the sword back in its sheath saying, "Here the sword (the storm) is in my Master's hands, that's why I'm not afraid."[77] His faith did not waver.

If we have the faith that the Master is with us in life as in death, should we be afraid to die?

Each day of our life must be lived in preparation for the inevitable encounter with death. But death need not be a stranger to us. We can meet it anywhere, anytime, if we are prepared.

The preparation is our daily meditation which should be a part of our being. Meditation is constant abandonment of the self, meditation is learning to die. Meditation is dying while living.

Shackles of Attachment

Detachment is death's pulse and heartbeat, prompting us to let go of the things we cling to. The tragedy of our struggle is our lack of acceptance and inability to let go. Acceptance of death seems unrealistic to us and altogether remote.

We may have been ill for years, yet our children, parents, brothers, sisters, spouses and friends are shocked when we die. There is always grief, melancholy, loneliness and confusion when someone passes away because we are terrified of letting go. We are terrified in fact of living, since learning to live is learning to let go.

Isn't it strange that despite the pain and suffering we go through in our lives, we rejoice at the birth of a newborn brought into this world, yet we weep endlessly at the death of someone who is finally rid of all the suffering?

Have we ever thought about this – why do we find it difficult to be alone in a room with a dead body for too long? Even if it is our father whom we once loved so much, the son who was the apple of our eye, the spouse we claimed we couldn't live without. This same father, son, or husband – now reduced to a corpse – fills us with uneasiness and discomfort.

A person may be lying in coma and we have no problem spending time with him. So why do we feel hesitation with a dead body? It's because the soul is missing. Unconsciously, unknowingly we loved the soul, not the body. When a person dies and the soul leaves the body, there is nothing left to love.

There is a story of a distraught woman who went to the Buddha because her child had died. She cried and begged the Buddha to revive her son.

The Buddha said, "Bring me a handful of mustard seeds – one seed from each house where no one has lost a child, husband, parent, or friend." Then I will revive your son.

She went searching and questioning house to house, village to village, but found that death had come to every family.

She went back to the Buddha and said, "I have not returned to you in order to revive my son. The child has gone. I will go and everyone will go. I realize now that death is a reality; it's the only certainty. I have come to you to initiate me into a life that never ends."

Everything decays. All relationships end. All attachments cease. In the face of death, detachment is the finale!

This has been summed up aptly by Sri Nisargadatta Maharaj: "Spiritual maturity lies in the readiness to let go of everything. The giving up is the first step. But the real giving up is in realizing that there is nothing to give up, for nothing is your own."[78]

Possessions, relationships and attachments are mere illusions; nothing is ours so there is nothing to give up. Only when we remove the shackles of attachment can we progress in our inner journey to the final liberation.

Clinging to Our Identity

> A river moves on, and by its own nature it is moving. But
> if you were to sit on a rock and paddle your feet in its
> water, it is for the sheer joy of it. But to feel and then to
> assert that your paddling is the cause for the entire river
> movement, it is the play of your ego.[79]

That's the same attitude we have towards death. We constantly
get stressed about:

What will happen without me?
How will my family survive without me?
What about my house, my dog, my car, my office?
I, me, mine! Our self-importance continues to grow.

But look around. A country doesn't stop functioning because
its president passes on, neither does an industry come to a
grinding halt because its chairman dies. Nor does our family
stop functioning if a member passes away.

No – life goes on! We grieve only temporarily. Nothing,
absolutely nothing stops life from moving on. It's like the waves
in the ocean: the movement continues, waves don't stand still.
Life is like the waves – it continues moving. Sometimes the
tide is high and sometimes it is low, but it continues to move,
to ebb and flow.

We too are constantly changing. We change from infants to
children, to youngsters, to adults and then to old age. Change
is happening every second. The cells in our body regenerate
or break down. The expressions on our faces shift with our
mood. Our eyesight fades, our hearing deteriorates, our teeth

decay – these are alarm bells to warn us that the days are ticking by and our time will soon be up.

It's time to turn our attention inwards instead of trying to reverse the aging process. If the Lord had wanted us to be young forever, he would have designed our bodies not to age. Aging is part of his grand scheme to help us realize that death is close at hand. But the ego doesn't rest.

The ego resists and tries to reverse the natural process of graceful aging. We are afraid of getting old. We try to camouflage our age by dying our hair, ironing out our wrinkles with botox and lifting our sagging body parts with surgical tucks. We defy nature by experimenting and indulging in coloured lenses and nose jobs. Unavoidable pains in the body creep up with the passage of time, leaving only memories of our youth and exuberance, which are replaced by aching knees and hip joints.

We put so much effort, time, and money into beautifying this body, which eventually will decay and die. Why not spend that precious time and effort beautifying the soul, which is ageless, timeless and limitless? We accumulate wealth and hoard material things that we can't take with us after death. Why not accumulate the only wealth which we can take with us, the wealth of meditation? When we expend our precious time and energy in meditation, then the colour of our hair and the wrinkles on our face will cease to matter. Suffering, sorrow and sickness remind us that our end is near.

The ego adds to our heavy load of false responsibilities. That ego is the only thing we need to get rid of. In our preparation for the final journey, in our effort to die while living, we need to overcome our fear, break away from the shackles of attachment and dissolve our ego once and for all.

Dare to Die

Just One More Second

What is the first step towards attaining enlightenment?

We need to form the habit of meditating every single day. To achieve our goal, to go towards the direction we are seeking, perseverance is absolutely necessary.

When the alarm goes off in the morning – in that one second we've made our choice! Just that one second determines our willpower, intention and love – or lack of it! Just that one second determines the intensity of our yearning and desire to reach the Ultimate. We can be up at the sound of the alarm or turn off the alarm and go back to sleep. Are we eager to begin our spiritual journey or not? In that one second we decide.

Now imagine a scenario when we plan a vacation –
Say we have a late night flight to catch.
We wouldn't need to set the alarm.
We'd probably stay up all night, too excited to sleep.
We'd be humming and smiling and bouncy on our feet.
Our bags would be packed and we'd be raring to go!
And this is a vacation – it will end in a week or two and then we'll be back in the same old grind.

Here's another scenario –
We've committed to undertake a journey to meet our Master.
We need to set the alarm.
When it rings we promptly turn it off and go back to sleep.
There's no excitement or eagerness, only yawns and snores.
Some days we lazily manage to lift ourselves partially out of bed.

From the sitting position we sneak back into the lying position, sleep undisturbed.

The Master waited, but we failed in our commitment.

The journey never started!

We didn't make it!

We lost the chance.

Sri Ramakrishna Paramahansa used to tell this story:

The Master was asked by his disciple: "How do we attain enlightenment?"

The Master and disciple went to a pond of water. There the Master pushed his disciple's head under water until he struggled to come up.

Gasping for breath, the disciple asked, "Why did you do that?"

The Master replied "That is how you attain enlightenment. When the yearning and intensity is so strong, like gasping for a breath of air, you will achieve it."[80]

Let's start our journey with the same yearning and intensity, like gasping for a breath of air.

Let's start by waking up!

Stilling the Body

The next step is to sit in a state of immobility, in a naturally comfortable way as shown to us at the time of initiation, or else the body will constantly remind us of its presence and draw our attention back to the external world. With the spine straight and eyes closed, we need to bring our attention to the eye centre. This process of stilling the body and focusing at the eye centre with continuous simran helps us to withdraw from the body's senses by slowly numbing them. The withdrawal starts from the toes upwards to the eye centre. Through simran, as the body becomes immune to all sensations, the attention becomes more and more focussed at the centre behind the eyes.

Stilling the body is certainly not easy. No doubt it is difficult at first, but we have to keep trying, for only practice makes perfect. Would a mother give up hope in trying to save her dying child? With fierce determination she would leave no stone unturned to try anything in this world to save her child. If we were held at gun point and told not to move – would we dare twitch? The fear would freeze us, turn us into statues. That is the firm resolve required to discipline ourselves – not out of fear but with perseverance. When we set out with a firm resolve to achieve our goal, we are already halfway to success.

Our desire has to be deep and desperate. Only if we have tremendous hunger and thirst for the truth can we find it. There are no half-measures in spirituality. It's all or nothing.

The well-known saying makes it clear: "It is not to question when or why, but only to do or die!"

Human achievement has far exceeded our expectations – after all, we have sent people to the moon. So it sounds ridiculous to say that we cannot discipline ourselves to sit still for a couple of hours each day. Has anyone achieved a reward without hard work? Doctors, lawyers, painters and musicians put in hours, days, months and years of dedicated practice to achieve their goals. They don't just sit back and make grandiose plans for being professionals. They worked hard and achieved.

This is what is needed:

Not accomplishment at first, but endeavour; not perfection at first, but effort; not certainly the showing out of the ideal, but the striving after it amid whatever failure and amid whatever error.[81]

Just Let Go

During meditation, we have to let go of our worldly burdens – thoughts of home, office, spouses, children, pets, and so forth. This is our special time with the Master, and no other thought should distract our attention. We must ignore the noise outside our room, whether the washing machine is on or the milk is boiling over or the dog hasn't been fed. We can never have a perfect situation; there is no such thing. The only perfect time is our time spent in meditation because that is our only time alone with the Master.

A disciple asked his Master: "Isn't the end-point of man's journey his union with God?"

The Master replied, "The end-point of man's journey is not union with God because there has never been a separation. All that is needed is the flash of insight that makes one see it."[82]

Are we ready for that flash of insight?

Meditation is a method by which we detach ourselves from this chaotic world by attaching ourselves to the divinity within. Meditation should be done without motive or expectation. We must remove the mind from all inside chatter and outside activity. Concentrated meditation is how we can lose our self by rising above all thoughts, desires, and passions.

Our journey begins when we collect our attention at the eye centre by means of *simran*, or repetition of the holy names we're given at the time of initiation. This process slowly calms the wavering mind. With the repetition of simran, the mind empties itself of chaotic thoughts and gradually becomes focussed at the eye centre. The simran helps in retaining one-pointed focus.

During simran, visualization of the physical form of the Master comes and goes in flashes before the mind. This visualization of the Master is *dhyan*. For example, when we refer to a friend in a conversation, the image of that person comes to our mind. When we think of a memorable incident, that image immediately comes up as a visual in the mind. So it is with simran and dhyan. When we sit in stillness and silence repeating simran, the form of the Master flashes through the mind because of our association with him.

At first, the image of the Master wavers, shakes, and comes and goes because our simran and concentration is not stable and firm. But once we are focused with one-pointed concentration and relentless perseverance during simran, the concentration stabilizes at the third eye – the *tisra til* or eye centre. During this stage of concentrated, deep contemplation, when the simran is firm, dhyan of the Master becomes a natural consequence. At this stage, the grace of the Master results in dhyan.

Bhajan. "Just let go," the Master says. When all thoughts cease to exist, when there is emptiness and darkness, when the mind becomes desireless and self-awareness is dissolved, the "I" dissipates. Without the "I," the mind is fathomless, limitless, and egoless. When the concentration is solidly rooted at the eye centre, a faint, distant melody is heard. In the silence of the mind it becomes clearer, melodic, and irresistible. The inward journey of the soul begins. The melody of the Shabd or Sound Current attracts the soul and pulls it up. At this point the radiant form of the Master engulfs the soul: "If thine eye be single, thy whole body shall be full of light."[83]

The Shabd, the sound and light, awakens the soul. The awakening of the soul is called "dying while living." When the mind and body are dead, the soul awakens and experiences bliss.

In that state of self-realization, the joy of the soul surpasses anything the mind and intellect can conceive of. The infinite magnitude of that experience is beyond human comprehension.

Just as a wild animal seeks its prey or a man dying of hunger craves for even a grain of food, with that same intensity, desperation, and single-mindedness, we should follow our desire for spiritual practice. Just let go – dare to die!

A beautiful story of Arjuna is told. He asked his Master, mentor and guide, Krishna, "You say great things. You argue well. But still doubts persist within me because I have not experienced what you talk about. Why don't you give me some experience so my doubts can disappear?"

Krishna agreed and in a flash, Krishna became huge. The worlds, stars, and planets started rotating around him; suddenly Krishna had millions of hands – it was chaos. Arjuna thought he was going mad and in fear he cried, "Please come back, please come back to your ordinary form. I am frightened."

Krishna came back to his ordinary form and said "I knew you were not ready."[84]

We want initiation today and enlightenment tomorrow!

Do the daily meditation and just let go, die while living, break away from the bondages of materialism, the chains of attachment; shake off those shackles poisoned with deadly passions. Meditation is rising above desires, worldly entanglements and attachments.

Let's dare to do it!

Let's dare to be brave and conquer our mind. Conquest lies in making the initial effort, for action breeds reaction. In the language of realization, the most valuable word is effort. A few failings don't matter. Remember, even though the clouds gather thick, beyond them the sun still shines.

We need to come out of our shells and be persistent and determined.

From this time on, we should grow – grow inwards, not outwards.

Just let go – dare to die!

Discipline of Discipleship

There was a disciple who stayed with his Master for many years. He became enlightened, but continued to stay with the Master. One day the Master said to him, "Now that you are enlightened, why do you continue to stay here?"

The disciple replied, "Unless you say so, how can I leave?" He continued to stay with the Master.

After a few years, the Master again said, "Why do you keep following me? Go and teach people."

The disciple replied, "You direct me and I will follow, for I am nothing without you."

This is so beautiful and true! A disciple is simply a follower, a shadow. Being a shadow is living in the Master's will. There is no other way of being a devoted disciple than being drenched in love, soaked to the core of one's being and living in his will. A true disciple remains a follower; he knows only how to live in the discipline of discipleship. The ultimate discipline is living in the Master's will. Unless the Master tells him to leave, he doesn't budge. When the Master instructs, "Go and teach people," the disciple says, "You direct me and I will follow." Whatever the Master directs him to do, he will do.

Resistance shakes up our equilibrium, whereas acceptance brings equanimity. We get disappointed and disillusioned when we try to impose our will on destiny. We should believe that whatever he is doing is for our best and highest good. That doesn't mean we won't undergo pain and pruning. Pain is often part of growth.

Guru Arjan Dev said:

tera kee'a meetha laagai.
har naam padaarath Nanak maangai.

Thine doings seem sweet unto me.
Nanak craves for the wealth of God's Nam.[85]

On being tortured to death, Guru Arjan Dev declared: "Sweet is thy will, O Lord."

And in the Bible we read: "Thy will be done in earth, as it is in heaven."[86]

As Baba Ji mentioned at a recent question-and-answer session, *"Aap ki arzi, uski marzi,"* meaning: You can ask, desire or want, but what he gives, how he gives, where he gives, when he gives or if he gives at all is all by his will.

The first discipline for a disciple is to stay in his will!

Anchored in Love

Love is a culmination of many feelings blended together that causes us to spontaneously and voluntarily submit to our beloved. We can't force this, it just happens. Love and submission are giving, giving in an egoless state so that we can blend with and mould ourselves to another.

Baba Ji says that love is to give, give and give!

In love we have no barriers, no expectations; we just give wholeheartedly. That is a state of submission, the highest expression of love.

To give in totality and transcend the self – only then can a disciple become one with the Master's true form.

No other love in any kind of relationship sinks so deep into the very core of our being. The love of a mother for her child, one spouse for another, one sibling for another or even for a friend – these relationships eventually wither away. Even the loss of a loved one loses its sting with the passage of time. None of these bonds are everlasting.

Take for instance the love of a mother for her child. Her child is the epitome of her existence. She feeds him, nurses him, loves and protects him. Similarly, for the child, his mother is the greatest mother in the world. He is totally dependent on her. She teaches him to speak his first word and lovingly watches while he takes his first step. The child learns to talk and walk, gets married, has his own children, quietly walking into his new life without his mother. The greatest mother in the world slowly gets reduced to a weekend visit, a Thanksgiving dinner or a Christmas lunch. As the son grows attached to his own little family, his priorities change and so does the intensity of his childhood love.

We live in countless fleeting relationships, seeking, finding, and losing. We take into ourselves our loved one's thoughts and voices; we absorb their presence and mannerisms, only to find that to expect perfect love in human relationships is folly.

Real love does not have ups and downs from time to time. We cannot love more today and less another day. We can't switch our emotions on and off. If true love exists then it will always remain. Love can only increase with each passing day. There is no limit to how much we can love.

The kind of love that holds us together, the one that is permanent, the one that encompasses our entire being, is a disciple's love for the Master.

It is said: "Bees, when caught in a storm in the fields, take up little stones to keep their balance in the air and not be easily carried away by the storm."[87]

So can we, by holding fast to our love for the Master, preserve our balance in the storms of change, whether temporal or spiritual, whether within or about us. Amid all the storms and changes in our lives, there is only one permanent relationship, that of the Master and disciple. That is the only one that will remain true, steadfast and eternal in this world and the next.

To love the Master unconditionally would be to eradicate the "I." True surrender is accepting wholeheartedly whatever comes from the Master, whether in the form of pain or joy. It is only after our ego is eradicated that we can experience real love.

A Sufi mystic said: "Love is an incurable disease – no one who catches it wants to recover, and all its victims refuse a cure."[88]

That is being anchored in love with the Master!

Live the Teachings

A disciple asked his Master, "What is your fundamental teaching?"

The Master said, "When it is hot, it is hot. When it is cold, it is cold."

The disciple was shocked. "What does that mean – when it is hot, it is hot, when it is cold, it is cold? What kind of philosophy is that?"

The Master said, "This is the whole of my philosophy: just live in the moment, whatever it may be – when it is hot, it is hot – don't desire the opposite. Accept."[89]

The Master can instruct only at the level of the disciple's understanding. His philosophy is simple; be desireless, accept everything – hot or cold, sun or rain.

The teachings are the foundations necessary for the disciple's spiritual development.

Just as a child cannot understand the attainments of a learned person, in the same way, a disciple cannot understand the Master. The Master is a paradox, an enigma! We can understand his teachings, not his ways. We make silly comparisons like, this did not happen during the Great Master's time or that was not so during Hazur Maharaj Ji's time, little realizing that the Master deals with present-day situations according to the needs of the changing times.

The Master's style, choice of words and actions can change to adapt to a new generation, but the teachings don't change. The Master is here to relate to us and that is possible only if he speaks to us in the language we understand. This does not mean the Master has to be a linguist. Speaking in our language means being able to relate to us in a manner that we can comprehend.

There is a peculiar power in the Master's words. His words have a force which the intellectual cannot always comprehend. When the Master speaks, it is his inner experience that speaks through him, not mere intellect. The arguments and interpretations coming from intellect, however beautiful and loaded with substance, cannot compare to the spoken words of a true Master.

No matter what words the Master uses, what language he speaks, or how long or short his satsangs, his message is the same. His message has never changed; his ultimate message is only one – meditation.

Of all our miseries, the most bitter is this: to understand so much and yet to have control over nothing. Just as we trust the doctor to cure us, trust the lawyer to get us justice, trust the bank to keep our money safe, we have to trust that the Master will step in and take charge of our lives. But that can happen only when we live in his teachings!

His Will or Nothing

These four simple words have a meaning way beyond our understanding. This is not a cliché. We need to understand that these words form the core of spiritual teachings.

The understanding and practice of living in his will is discipleship. Discipleship is discipline, discipline is obedience, obedience is surrender – and surrender is living in his will. The consequence and enormity of surrender can make a sinner into a saint, because surrender, or living in his will, is enlightenment.

"May the will of Allah be done," a pious man said.
"It always is, in any case," said Mullah Nasruddin.
"How can you prove that, Mullah?" asked the man.
"Quite simply, if it wasn't always being done by his will, then surely at some time or another my will would be done, wouldn't it?"[90]

It is said: "Surrender is the most difficult thing in the world when you are doing it; and the easiest when it is done."[91] Surrender is a state of an unquestioning mind coupled with implicit trust. Surrender is not a demand made by a Master; it is a natural consequence of a disciple's devotion.

The stumbling block in the way of surrender comes from our so-called knowledge and intelligence, which consist of theories, words, doctrines and dogmas. We can collect fragments of knowledge from here and there and become encyclopaedias, but for those in search of truth, knowledge becomes a huge barrier.

When we shed outer knowledge and learning and empty the mind, then we can experience the true knowing. This comes from inner experience. Only on that level can we claim to know.

Here is a beautiful story of Buddha's way of teaching:

The Buddha asked Ananda to get water from the stream. The stream was filled with dirty water and Ananda thought it was not appropriate for the Master to drink it, so he returned without the water. Buddha sent him again.

Ananda thought, why is the Master repeatedly sending me back when I have informed him that the water is dirty? So he went back again without the water.

Buddha sent him a third time. This time Ananda thought he would wait for the water to settle. He spent a few hours by the stream waiting for the dirt to settle, so the water would be clear for the Master to drink.

Sitting in the silence, he understood the Master's message to him. He realized what his Master was teaching him, that the stream is like our mind – we need to wait patiently, watch the mind carefully, let it settle down, and things will slowly get clearer. When the mind stops fluttering, it enters into a peaceful space, into a state of awareness and then surrender.[92]

The Sufi saint Rabia of Basra prayed to the Lord:

O my Lord, whatever share of this world Thou does bestow on me, bestow it on Thine enemies, and whatever share of the next world Thou dost give me, give it to Thy friends. Thou art enough for me.[93]

Pain of Separation

The pain of separation is like the poison of a cobra. Once it enters anyone's heart, it is not possible to get rid of it by any means unless one meets the Master. There is no other method.[94]

Maharaj Sawan Singh

Separation is double-edged: joyful yet painful; unbearable, yet we don't want to be rid of it; it brings our being alive yet kills it. The duality of ecstasy, fervour, and yearning, coupled with agony, obsession and angst – this feverish madness, uncontrollable craving, and unstoppable helplessness is the desire of the soul to unite with the Master's radiant form.

No words can describe the pain of separation. It's like a knife tearing apart every nerve and vein in the body. Every moment in separation cuts deep to the core, every cell in the body cries and reaches out, wanting to be one again with the beloved. It is impossible to express.

There is a poignant story about the renowned Sufi saint Bulleh Shah. Owing to his ego and pride, he suffered years of painful separation from his Master.

Bulleh Shah's Master, Inayat Shah, belonged to a low caste, while Bulleh Shah belonged to a high caste. Bulleh Shah invited his Master to a family wedding.

Bulleh Shah was disappointed that his Master did not attend the wedding himself, but sent one of his poorest disciples to represent him. Embarrassed by the disciple's dress and appearance, Bulleh Shah paid no attention to him. On his return, the disciple informed Inayat Shah that Bulleh Shah had completely ignored him at the wedding. On hearing this, the Master felt that by doing so, Bulleh Shah had disrespected him, not the disciple. The Master saw that Bulleh Shah still had a lot of arrogance and pride left in him.

Thereafter, he refused to meet Bulleh Shah despite his desperate efforts to meet his Master. According to history, for twelve long years, Bulleh Shah tried unsuccessfully to mend the rift with his Master. It is in those long years of painful separation that he wrote his haunting poetry on yearning and forgiveness.

One day, when Bulleh Shah heard that his Master was going to visit his village, he put aside his pride and joined the dancing girls. When Inayat Shah arrived at the village, Bulleh dressed like a woman and, drenched in love, sang in praise of his Master, dancing on the streets of the village in sheer madness, seeking his Master's forgiveness. Everyone around him thought that he had gone mad, and so he had. He was oblivious to the mocking of the crowd – the more they jeered at him, the more intoxicated he became in his love for his Master. He wanted only to earn his Master's forgiveness and win back his love.

Not recognizing Bulleh in a woman's attire, the Master asked, "Are you Bulleh?" "No," he cried, "I am *bhullah*," meaning, "I am the lost one."

Such was his longing to be with his Master! We realize the true intensity of such a love only when we are separated from our beloved.

In separation, we feel immense joy in our pain. We want the pain to continue. Tears may keep flowing, yet tears are not enough. Words are worthless. The mind remains in a state of madness.

This is the same yearning and longing, the same *birha* and *nasha*, the same love and devotion that should consume our being in our desire to see the Master's radiant form. Every nerve and cell in our body should be aching and pushing us towards the Master's inner form. Until we see him within, we will continue to feel intense pain, this *tarap*, longing and yearning.

Hazur Maharaj Ji often explained to us, "The more the pain of separation, the greater the intensity of our love!"

And the present Master says, "You have to lose yourself – to be found!"

Darshan Phenomena

Darshan is the result of deep, intense love. When our eyes are riveted towards the Master without conscious effort; when we are paralyzed and awestruck by his aura; when we are drawn towards him like a needle to a magnet; when we are so engrossed and absorbed by his presence that the world comes to a standstill and nothing else matters; when the pull is so strong and uncontrollable that we are oblivious of everything around us – that is darshan.

But we run around from one "darshan" to another without truly absorbing the enormity and relevance of the Master's presence. We elbow our way to satsang to grab the best seats and wait with bated breath for the Master to arrive, and whoa... five minutes into satsang and we are shamelessly yawning or nodding off, as though the Master had spread a sleeping sickness amongst us. We fall asleep at meditation, we fall asleep in his presence, we feel constantly starved of sleep – yet we effortlessly stay up for hours watching movies or indulging in worldly pursuits.

The Master sits through the entire satsang patiently waiting, waiting for those to whom he can give darshan, picking out the ones who are ready to receive, but all he sees are sleeping beauties or cluttered minds. How can he give darshan if we shut ourselves off from him? How can he give when we have not prepared ourselves to receive his darshan, by emptying our mind and filling it with simran and meditation?

We've been sleeping all our lives, and he is here to awaken us from this sleep state. If we truly understood the significance of darshan, we would not be able to breathe, let alone close our eyes and fall asleep. His presence should be so intoxicating that it awakens every nerve, fibre and cell in our body and mind so that we can absorb his divine aura – but that is possible only if we have done our meditation!

Every time we hope to get darshan without doing our meditation, we have lost that darshan, lost that opportunity. We are unable to receive because our minds are not focused towards our goal. We've missed what he came to give; we've missed what we came to receive.

Darshan is not just staring at the Master – it's about receptivity. When we don't put in the time and effort in bhajan and simran, we inadvertently build a wall around us where the radiance or power of darshan cannot penetrate. Without meditation we block ourselves so that we are unable to receive when the Master desperately wants to give us.

So let's remove those blocks, demolish the wall and prepare ourselves – by doing bhajan and simran. Then when we sit before the Satguru, we will be able to immerse ourselves in his grace, aura and presence.

During darshan we are not to concentrate on the Master's turban, beard, hands, facial features, shoes or clothes – darshan is absorbing the aura, radiance, and purity of the Master's presence. Baba Ji constantly reminds us that dhyan (inner contemplation on his form) is not within our power; it is given by the Master. During dhyan, it's the aura and purity of the Master that we experience. The physical imagery during dhyan is a way to reassure and guide us because that form is familiar to us. But eventually, the Master's inner form is pure light; his magnificence is in the form of a radiant, powerful light, not in his physical appearance.

During darshan, a miracle transpires, something esoteric that cannot be expressed in words. The presence of a Master is a living experience every moment!

Darshan of the Master by a seeker is the Master's subtle enticement and seduction of his marked sheep into the fold. He lights the first spark of desire, hunger and thirst in a seeker with his magnetism. He creates within the seeker a curiosity for the Lord. The Master's presence rivets the seeker with his captivating energy.

The Master does not ask for anything and neither does he impose. He does not coerce anyone; rather he encourages seekers to question till they are completely at ease and confident that this is the path they want to follow. He waits patiently for a seeker to clear his doubts and satisfy his curiosity before committing himself to the spiritual path. Seekers are advised to read books, hear satsangs, and even read critical comments about the path before deciding whether they are ready to embark on this journey.

During darshan a seeker is drawn to the mesmerizing energy and mysterious nature of the Master. He hopes the Master's spiritual power, attained through inner experience, will be transmitted to him. Just as a flame jumps from a lit lamp to an unlit lamp, the same happens between a Master and seeker – transmission beyond words, beyond scriptures, a transmission of indisputable energy!

Darshan of the Master by an initiate strengthens the bond between the Master and disciple, a culmination of the disciple's obedience to the commitment to meditate. It is also the

Master's appreciation and acknowledgment of the disciple's effort at meditation.

Darshan is the Master's acceptance of the disciple's submission. Darshan is the Master's reciprocation of the disciple's trust and faith in him, an offering of reassurance that he is there to see his disciples through their spiritual journey and remove any obstacle encountered on the way.

Darshan is a two-way street – it's like looking at our reflection in a mirror – he is there because we were there, in meditation. He gives because he knows we are prepared to receive. Darshan forges an indescribable bond between a Master and disciple.

Satsang Is an Appetizer

Through these haunting lines, Hazur Maharaj Ji explains the relationship between satsang, meditation, and love:

> Going to satsang is an act of devotion.
> Meditation is an act of love.
> You cannot reach love without devotion.
> Therefore, satsang leads and love is born.[95]

The importance of attending satsang could not be made clearer. Satsang is like a warm-up exercise to help us live the day in an atmosphere of love and remembrance of the teachings. It is an aid to help us focus in the right direction; to keep our minds inclined towards spirituality and the method to attain the goal.

Sri Ramakrishna Paramahansa explains: "The soul that is wholly world-bound is like the worm that lives in filth forever, and dies in it not knowing any better. The soul whose worldliness is of lesser intensity is, however, like the fly that sometimes sits now on filth and now on sugar. The free soul alone is like the bee that always drinks honey and nothing else."[96]

Discipline at Satsang

No matter what seva we do, no matter how indispensable we think we may be, none of us here are too busy to arrive at satsang on time. This is not a place to make a grand entrance, to show off our supposed importance. Sitting together is a reminder that we are all beggars in his court, pleading for his grace and mercy. We are here to be reminded about where we are headed and how to get there. And punctuality is the first discipline. No seva can be important enough or a good enough excuse for being late for satsang.

At the Dera, when we arrive at satsang, the first thought that consumes us is the desire to sit in front. Baba Ji has often said that if we really believed that the Master is all knowing, we would not be able to sit in front of him at all. It is also explained that each one of us will get what we come for. Those of us who want to be noticed, to sit in front –that is all we will receive because that is the extent of our receptivity. Those who come for spiritual wealth sit anywhere and receive all – because their minds are focused only in that direction.

The Master shows us the attitude we should have during satsang – concentration of the mind and stillness of the body. At satsang we see the Master sitting absolutely still day after day – we need to imbibe that same quality of physical discipline.

Time and again we are reminded that after satsang at the Dera, we should wait for "Radha Soami" to be said before we get up from our seats. But we're in a tearing hurry to get up and leave, as if we can't stand sitting still for one more minute. With little or no concern for the elderly and infirm, we elbow our way through the crowd, consumed only with ourselves, unable to discipline ourselves to obey simple instructions.

At satsang we are reminded of our true identity. Who we are and where we come from is unimportant. Whether we are politicians, professionals, industrialists, farmers, or housewives, the Master sees us as being all the same. He does not see the colour of our skin or hair, whether we're young or old, fat or thin, man or woman, rich or poor, beautiful or scarred, if we have one limb or four. To the Master we are his souls, in the Master's eyes, we are all equal.

Attendance at Satsang

Our attendance at satsang should not depend on the Master's physical presence alone. Our love for him should be such that we feel his presence within us even in his absence. If we believe he is everywhere, then we must also believe that he is here even when he is not. Let's get this straight: the Master does not need to hear satsang; he comes to instil a certain discipline in us. Satsang is for us – we need it.

There is no doubt that there is a difference when the Master is not there. At Dera, seeing his empty seat at satsang rips our hearts to pieces. But his absence should not deter us from attending satsang. Our need for satsang is greater in his absence because we are at our weakest then. When we find out that the Master will not be at satsang, we say, "Oh! I don't have to go to satsang today." Well, we don't have to go today or tomorrow or ever. Our need should bring us here; if we cannot condition ourselves to giving forty-five minutes to satsang for inspiration, how can we expect to give time to meditation?

Hazur Maharaj Ji made the importance of satsang very clear when he said: "Satsang is an appetizer to create real hunger for the darshan of the Lord."[97]

Repetition of the Teachings

We often hear people say that the same things are repeated at every satsang – but of course, they have to be repeated. When the teachings never change, how can they not be repeated? Besides, have we attained such a level of spirituality that we do not need to be reminded of the teachings, reminded of the very source and foundation of our beliefs? The repetition is to give us a solid foundation.

How many times in nursery school were we told to repeat ABC? From the time a child is able to decipher sounds, those three letters are drummed into his ears. Until a child is fully conversant with A to Z, he is not taught anything else.

Our focus needs constant pulling. That's why we need to hear the same things repeatedly, to let it register in our minds. We are taught to keep our simran flowing 24/7 – we don't ask for the five names to change every few months because we tire of repeating the same mantra over and over again. It is not like a combination to a vault or computer password that we can change from time to time. The power of the words is instrumental in our journey within.

Likewise, hearing the same things at satsang reminds us of our goal. The message doesn't change but the way it is expressed may differ. The teachings are simple and straightforward and there is only one message to give, so naturally it will be repeated.

Satsangs are our spiritual education, to teach us the basics and move us along to achieve the Ultimate!

Baba Ji's
Famous One-Liners

Baba Ji is a master of making deep statements and giving invaluable answers with just a few words. He is brief, precise, to the point. The one-liners on the following pages hold volumes of depth, understanding through personal experience, and inexpressible inner wisdom!

Everything Is Parshad

Now here is a perfect example of a fool, the fool that is the analytical human mind!

This foolish disciple asks the Master, "You say 'everything is parshad,' then why do we have the special blessing on parshad distribution day? And if everything is parshad, then why have parshad at all?" By our standards, that's an intelligent question, right? And the foolish mind thinks, "Well, let me hear what the Master has to say to that one."

But the Master has a smile on his lips and a twinkle in his eye as he repeats: "Everything is parshad." That leaves the fool more confused than ever. The Master in his usual impish way gives food for thought and plants the seed of awareness. The first step towards awareness is to recognize that in spirituality, intelligence and knowledge are worthless. We think with our mind, we use our intelligence, while the Master talks from another level, from the spiritual level. He speaks from the highest realms; therefore we miss his message. Its simplicity passes us by because we rely on our mind. As Hazur Maharaj Ji used to say, we can't understand simple things in a simple way.

Master says, "Everything is parshad," and we don't understand his words. We only see the gesture and forget the words. We cling to the superficial because we are accustomed to material rewards and cannot break free from these shackles. Our concepts and perceptions are narrow, so we think we are being given parshad for having done something unique or special. We expect an incentive for everything we do, even seva. He indulges us. He gives us a packet of parshad to satisfy our need for worldly goodies – material expressions of his love – thus allowing us to bask in the ecstasy of our illusions.

Instead of receiving parshad as a way to remember the Master and his blessings, we concoct myths and stories about its meaning. Our materialism and our narrow concepts and beliefs limit our understanding. We send parshad to the sick hoping they will get better; feed it to our children so they too might follow the spiritual path. Do we really think that "faith-healing" people and "converting" others by giving them parshad is our purpose in life? Such confused souls!

What then is parshad? The outside parshad is but a minute sample of what awaits us inside. He is enticing us, giving us the bait, luring us to take the ultimate gift where "everything is parshad." He wants us to look beyond the physical; he wants us to look deep within. Whatever is given to us by the Lord is parshad – your body, your health, your every breath is parshad. He says, if the outside parshad gives us so much joy and happiness, come and receive the parshad inside; experience the gift of inner bliss.

Everything is bliss inside, therefore "everything is parshad." The inner bliss will wash away the things we give importance to in the physical. He is urging us to go in and realize that the outside desires are meaningless. Inside there will be nothing to know because we will be all-knowing, there will be nothing to ask because there will be nothing left to gain, there will be no desire because there will be no attachment. So he says, look inside, where everything is nothing but that nothingness is everything – where everything is parshad.

Cornering the Master

The doubting, analytical mind, the foolish disciple, asks the Master: "You tell us to ask questions, not to have blind faith. But faith *is* blind." Then we arrogantly sit back to hear the Master's response, thinking: now I've cornered the Master!

Ha! So now this fool is trying to teach the Master by reversing roles. Listen carefully: "While the world says, "All faith is blind," the Master says, "don't follow blindly." The Master challenges the world by declaring the opposite, contradicts a commonly accepted belief and thoroughly confuses us, throwing us into a total dilemma. Then he happily sits back and says, with childlike innocence, "I am here to confuse you." Ya, right!

Wait a minute, we think: he's not supposed to confuse us; he's supposed to anchor us. But the Master has his own mysterious ways; he anchors us through confusion. While the others say, anchor yourself to remove the confusion, the Master says the opposite: get confused and then you will be anchored. He confuses us to a point where we finally, through sheer exhaustion, drop this mind and say, "Okay, have it your way! I give up." And that is precisely the moment he is waiting for, for us to give in. That's why he encourages us to question. He wants us to reach a point of surrender. He makes us so confused that we get exhausted and say, "We give up and give in."

The Masters never change their teaching. Their words, their teachings, make us change.

What the Master is teaching us here is that even though faith is blind, in a sense, we do not have the power to follow blindly. So he says, ask questions, keep asking questions till your mind is insane, ask till you have no more left. When you start following the path, your questions automatically will be resolved.

Questions come out of doubts and confusion. It is the doubting mind that forces us to analyze and dissect. If we truly had blind faith, we would have no questions. We ask on the intellectual level and he answers on the spiritual level.

He indulges us because he is preparing us for the final purification. So he says, "Ask questions," burn yourself out, drive the mind so insane that eventually we just give up. He is preparing us to break free and fly, to wake up to our true potential.

He sees in us that potential. That's why he insists that we clear the doubts not through answers but through a multitude of questions, because when the mind is in turmoil, frantically analyzing, asking, churning, running wild and loose, it reaches a point of complete exhaustion – and because there are no answers on the outside, it gives up. And that is exactly the point the Master is waiting for, for us to give up and give in, so he can start the process of purification.

The purification is a point when the mind drops and we enter a deep silence. When the mind discovers how to be still it becomes silent, and in the silence nothing remains. When the mind surrenders to silence there are no waves, no wavering, only calmness and serenity. The Master wants us to exhaust the mind to a point of stillness, so we can experience the silence within. That is our true initiation – inner experience through silence. In that silence, there will be no questions. You will be transformed.

Gimme, Gimme, Gimme...

Again the foolish mind constantly badgers the Master saying, "Master, I can't meditate, please give me your grace, your *daya*, your *mehr*." Every disciple has the same boring plea: just give give give because I want want want. As though grace is a thing he will pull out of his pocket and hand over to us, which we can then proudly take home and hang on the wall, or place on a table so we can admire it and others can too. In our materialism, we treat grace as a commodity. But he has already given his grace by initiating us – he cannot give more grace than that; on the physical level he can do no more.

Initiating us is the Master's ultimate grace! On this physical level, once he initiates us, his work is over, complete, *khatam* (finished). After that, our work starts – now we have to prepare ourselves to go within and receive the grace inside, which is the only place it can be given and received. The Master is not about to meditate for us. Showing the way to meditation is his work, but doing the meditation is our work.

"Master, I can't meditate, please give me your grace." Can we visualize the Master hearing this line maybe one hundred times a day, every single day? We'd be cooling our heels in a loony bin if we were badgered in the same way. The Master goes through it every single day. And each one of us who asks fancies it is the most unique question the mind has ever fashioned. And the Master listens indulgently, as though it *were* the most unique question in the world. We must be his most persistently boring experience ever.

Yet, the Master explains patiently: "What is so difficult about meditation? Just sit, close your eyes, and you will be there." We laugh, giggle and tell others about it, saying the Master has a great sense of humour. But the joke is on us – the intensity of his words bounce off us; we are unbelieving, because we lack trust in the Master's words.

He says, just sit still, remove yourself from worldly senses and distractions of the world, close your eyes, bring the attention to the eye centre, focus with single-mindedness, and you will be there.

Where is "there"? "There" is not here, it is the eye centre. He says, uproot your attention from here, from the physical, remove the passions and senses from here and you will be "there," inside. What's so difficult about that? he asks. What is so difficult about meditation? Just sit still, close your eyes, detach your thoughts and you will be there – die here and live there! What's so difficult about that? Don't be here; be there. Don't be dead; be alive. Dare the mind. Challenge it. Kill it. Conquer it. Just reach there...and witness his grace in abundance!

The Walking Stick

After Louise Hilger's death, Baba Ji went to her apartment to give instructions for the renovations. Standing on the balcony, he lifted her walking stick and raised it playfully as if to hit a *sevadarni* (a lady sevadar). Then he looked down from the balcony at the many Westerners collected on the lawn; all the heads were looking upwards at him in silence and awe. With the stick in his hand, ready for the blow, he silently and playfully, through his gestures, asked the Westerners below, "Shall I hit her?" In equal silence, all the heads spontaneously, in unison and without hesitation, bobbed, "Yes!" Everyone waited in anticipation, but he gently gave the stick to the sevadarni saying, "Keep it, you will need it." There were gasps and squeals of laughter. Everyone was happy to see the Master in such a playful mood.

But Baba Ji's play-acting had a deeper meaning.

"Shall I hit her?

And then, "Keep it, you will need it."

Most satsangis would keep the walking stick framed on their wall, announcing to everyone that Baba Ji had given it to them; it would undoubtedly become their most treasured possession. But it was not a material gift he gave. The stick has no value by itself, and of course he never would have actually hit the sevadar.

We could see the stick as a symbol for meditation, while the action of hitting is a reminder to follow the *hukam* of meditation. Because we do not stay with our commitment, he is hard pressed to make us realize through various ways to grab the opportunity, so he says, grab the stick, the meditation. Stay with the commitment, otherwise the hit – the blows, knocks and adversities – will be far more tedious to bear.

By giving the stick to the sevadarni, saying, "Keep it, you will need it!" he graciously reminds us of the need to meditate. He is not giving a material gift; he is warning us to keep the meditation flowing regularly – because we will need it – to anchor us. We will need the meditation as a shield, a buffer, to hold us together during the many calamities in our lives.

Keep a Balance

The Master says the simplest things with the deepest meaning.

Keep a balance: in these words he has compressed a multitude of actions, words and thoughts.

Our emotions tend to either soar or plummet. So the Master advises us to be balanced, steady and stable, stay rooted to an anchor. Stop rocking and swaying or we will blow with the wind and drift away.

The Master advises us live a householder's life, but with detachment. When we first come on the path, we put our life totally out of gear. In our excitement, we suddenly want to be *sadhus* and *sanyasis* – ascetics and renunciates. We want to run off to a cave or shut ourselves in a room so that we can meditate all day. We make excuses and run away from our responsibilities.

But the Master cautions us to keep a balance, to live a normal life and fulfil our responsibilities. He advises us to live with detachment, and weave meditation into our everyday lives.

Too much suppression causes the mind to rebel. Senses which are suppressed when we are isolated, for example, become heightened when we move away from that environment. Any extreme causes our system to revolt. Therefore we need to maintain a balance.

That is why Baba Ji says, don't swing to extremes; follow the middle path and be moderate.

We can be meditative yet joyous.

We can like and dislike, but without going to the extremes of love and hate.

We can be annoyed, but not to the point of seeking vengeance.

We can be committed to seva, yet at the same time remain committed to family responsibilities.

We can be natural – laugh and cry, sing and dance, contemplate and chatter, be silent and express ourselves – while living within the teachings. There is no contradiction!

We just need to be moderate and keep a balance.

Be an ordinary person, live an ordinary life. Just make meditation a part of the ordinary routine and retain a balance.

When we overeat, we vomit; when we diet, we get weak; and when we starve, we die – all extremes!

So Baba Ji says, keep a balance – don't swing like a pendulum. Extremes cause reactions; just follow the middle path.

Burn the Books

Baba Ji says with great panache, "Burn the books." While we are probably conjuring up ideas of a bonfire outside the library, he goes racing ahead and publishes more and more books.

"Burn the books"? He certainly knows how to get our attention. Baba Ji is telling us that books can give us knowledge and inspiration, but they can't replace experience – that's why eventually they aren't necessary.

Our dependence on book knowledge should not become a deterrent to our meditation. Words and theories are inconsequential. If the inspiration we get from the Sant Mat books is not put in action, then what use are they? If books are not inspiring us to meditate, then stop reading them; instead concentrate on the meditation.

Sometimes Baba Ji's words confuse us because we insist on using our intellect to try to understand them. We seem to enjoy these mind games. But in the depths of our confusion, we eventually give up trying to understand anything and the mind begins to settle down; and when the mind is calm we are able to understand his words more clearly.

We cannot use the books or our intellect to unravel the path to God-realization – only meditation can achieve that. We read books and say they are beautiful, but if the beauty of the words is not helping us achieve the ultimate, then stop reading. Book knowledge is useless after a point, only action via meditation is important. That's why Baba Ji says, "Burn the books."

A story is told about Rabindranath Tagore, the famous poet. Wanting to spend time reading in a quiet environment, he went to a forest for a few days.

One evening he was reading in candlelight when the wind extinguished the candle flame. He sat gazing at the moon, the stars and sky. Awed by the beauty around him, he realized what he had missed. He wrote in his diary, "The beauty can be seen, can be felt, can be experienced: it can drive you mad, but you cannot define it. And I decide from today not to read any book which is an effort to define beauty, because no book can do it."

Spirituality can be absorbed only in silence; language can never get to its essence, its depth, its beauty. Only experience, not knowledge, brings understanding.

Follow or Be Dragged

Baba Ji's most famous one-liner, and easily the scariest: "Follow or be dragged."

Now, who dares to ignore this warning given by the Master himself, particularly when he offers us a far easier, simpler solution – "Follow!" The meaning of "follow" is clear – live in his will, his *hukam*. Just one simple action – follow, obey the *hukam* of meditation.

Following the Master's *hukam* will give us the wisdom to face a multitude of adversities. Without the anchor of meditation, our lives will be like a stormy sea, so he says, "Follow," or meditate – for it will spare us from being "dragged."

The Master's primary work here is to get his souls back to their eternal home. He is going to do it; there is no stopping him. So we can either follow by living in the discipline of the Sant Mat teachings or our lives will be like the turbulent river that is knocked off its course. Likewise, we may have to be knocked around to bring us back on course. This clearly warns us that our journey on the physical and internal levels will be rough and tough without daily meditation.

If we want to be able to withstand adversity and remain balanced amidst the outside turmoil, we have to be rooted in our spiritual practice So obey the *hukam* and "follow"; or bear the consequences of living in turbulence and being "dragged."

The Master will drag us out from the deepest sea and from the highest mountain; we are his disciples, and we he won't give up on us. The Master gives us strength to cope with any crisis, but he will not change our destiny. He will not change the course; he will change us – whether we are willing or not.

He will ensure that we are freed from the shackles of this illusionary world, so there is nowhere for us to run or hide.

We can follow his lead willingly and enjoy the journey, or he can make it really tough for us! Choose between the two – surrender or suffer! Live in his will or suffer and be dragged from here to eternity.

He has a one-point agenda: to ensure that by hook or by crook we start the journey home. He is our redeemer, our saviour and our liberator. He will grind our mind to pulp and drag us along with him if we don't surrender and follow him. So don't be dragged, just follow! It is less painful.

The Magic Word

To every question the answer is the same. To every problem the answer is the same. Whether we ask for joy, grace, forgiveness, relief from pain or sickness, – there is a firm one-word answer – "meditate." Sometimes we wonder: How can the answer or solution to everything be meditation?

But if he says so, it must be! The power of daily meditation is inexpressible for those who practise it, because they feel the sea change within. Those who don't practise will continue to complain. Meditation works like a security blanket; it stabilizes the mind and prepares us to face adversities with courage and strength. Meditation is our responsibility, no one can help us there, it has to be an individual's effort – no one can wave a magic wand to make us sit.

Yet we want instant results. But in meditation we cannot expect an annual score card advising us of our progress. Judging our progress is not our concern. We have been told simply to meditate – just that – with no expectations, no rewards, no scores. Just sit every single day. But we want initiation today and expect enlightenment tomorrow. He says "meditate" and we interpret it as "enlightenment." That is the huge difference between what he says and how we misinterpret his words. When we claim we can't meditate, what we are saying is we are not getting enlightened.

The first step in our spiritual journey is meditation. Meditation purifies the mind and prepares the soul to attain enlightenment: God-realization. Meditation, purification, then enlightenment!

By insisting on "meditation" as the solution to every problem, Baba Ji is driving home the fact that daily meditation is a process which slowly detaches us from the physical by attaching us to the spiritual. This process of detachment helps us deal with everyday pains of life because we no longer let them get under our skin. It works as a shock-absorber during turbulent times. The awareness we get through meditation brings equanimity and gives us strength.

A disciple asked his Master "Can you say something about God?"

The Master replied, "Meditate."

The disciple was aghast: "Just this much, one word?"

The Master again said, "Meditate."

The disciple was puzzled, "You keep repeating yourself."

The Master again said, "Meditate. Nothing more can be said about it. You have to do it. You will have to do it."

Do it!

Dear Master –

There are so many religions that there must be that many gods, but we are told there is only one.

There are many photographs of various gods, but no one can confirm what he, the one God, really looks like.

No one has seen him, yet we hear he sneaks in to watch all our activities.

No one who has died has come back to earth to inform us about what he wears, what he looks like, what diet he fancies, or even about his preferences in movies and music.

We have no idea what language he speaks because he never speaks with words; we can only indulge in a monologue with him.

We can't call him, as his mobile number is unlisted.

He can't hear us because the satellites installed on earth don't connect with his.

We hear he has a kingdom, but it has no address.

God made us in his image, but now he hides himself, so we can't nag him about the imperfections of this world.

We cannot locate him on Facebook, Twitter or WhatsApp.

He's supposed to be all-forgiving – so what's the deal with the karma syndrome?

It's also said that he's all-knowing – but he doesn't seem to know that we can't find him with our eyes closed.

He schedules meetings at 3:00 am. Does that mean he's an insomniac?

He is called omni-present – but for us he's omni-absent.

We are told to "die while living," and then eventually we die — but when do we get to actually live?

He plays hide-and-seek with confused satsangis, saying, "Hey, find me within." But surely it would cause a stampede if we all rushed in together at three in the morning!

Since he is only one, wouldn't it be more reasonable if he just revealed himself to us instead?

— From your confused satsangis

To New Beginnings...

ENDNOTES

RSSB refers to books published by Radha Soami Satsang Beas.

1. Based on story retold in Osho, *The Hidden Harmony: Talks on Heraclitus*; Cologne: Rebel Publishing House, 2nd ed., 1991, ch. 5.
2. Bible, *1 Corinthians*, 3:16.
3. *The Complete Works of Nichiren Daishonin*, "On Attaining Buddhahood in This Lifetime," vol. I, p. 3; *http://www.nichirenlibrary.org/en/wnd-1/Content/1* (Ret. Nov. 2015).
4. Upanishads, Sixth Ayadhya, #11, p. 263–264; *http://www.sacred-texts.com/hin/sbe15/sbe15105.htm* (Ret. Nov. 2015).
5. Guru Arjan Dev, Adi Granth, p. 102.
6. Based on Idris Shah, ed., *The Exploits of the Incomparable Mulla Nasruddin*; London: Idris Shah Foundation, 1966, 2014, p. 9.
7. Bulleh Shah, *Kulliyat*, kafi 76, 157–159; in J. R. Puri & T. R. Shangari, *Bulleh Shah*; Beas, Punjab: RSSB, 2010, p. 64.
8. Guru Arjan Dev, Adi Granth, p. 293.
9. Guru Nanak, Adi Granth, p. 59.
10. Guru Amar Das, Adi Granth, p. 1044.
11. Thomas a Kempis, *The Imitation of Christ*, tr. G. F. Maine; London: Collins Publishers, 1957, 1971, ch. 56.
12. V. K. Sethi, *Kabir, Weaver of God's Name*; Beas, Punjab: RSSB, 1994, p. 207.
13. Guru Nanak, Adi Granth, p. 466.
14. Guru Arjan Dev, Adi Granth, p. 134.
15. Bible, *John*, 3:3.
16. *Sayings of Ramakrishna*, #94; *http://www.sacred-texts.com/hin/rls/rls25.htm* (Ret. Nov. 2015).

17. Guru Angad Dev, Adi Granth, p. 463.
18. As recounted in the satsangs of Hazur Maharaj Charan Singh and the present Master.
19. *Legacy of Love*; Beas, Punjab: RSSB, 2000, p. 547.
20. Hazrat Inayat Khan, *The Sufi Message of Hazrat Inayat Khan: The Vision of God and Man, Confessions, Four Plays*, vol. 12 of *The Sufi Message of Hazrat Inayat Khan*; Geneva: International Headquarters of the Sufi Movement, 1974, p. 105.
21. Henry T. Hamblin, in Andy Zubko, ed., *Treasury of Spiritual Wisdom*; San Diego: Blue Dove Press, 1998, p. 328.
22. Kabir, *Kabir Sakhi Sangrah*, p. 2:10 (tr. *Santon ki Bani*, RSSB, forthcoming).
23. Meher Baba, in Andy Zubko, ed., *Treasury of Spiritual Wisdom*; San Diego: Blue Dove Press, 1998, p. 264.
24. Willilam Shakespeare, *As You Like It*, act II, scene VII.
25. Daryai Lal Kapur, *Call of the Great Master*; Beas, Punjab: RSSB, 1989, p. 196.
26. *The Complete Works of Swami Vivekananda*, vol. 1; Calcutta: Advaita Ashrama, 2005, p. 142.
27. Kabir, Adi Granth, p. 1159.
28. Maharaj Charan Singh, *Spiritual Perspectives*, vol. I; Beas, Punjab: RSSB, 2010, p. 191.
29. Statement attributed to the Buddha; *http://www.slideshare.net/xingledout/reaping-what-you-sow-looking-at-karma-through-the-lens-of-thai-literature* (Ret. Nov. 2015), p. 4.
30. Bible, *Galatians*, 6:7.
31. Maharaj Charan Singh, *Die to Live*; Beas, Punjab: RSSB, q. 25.
32. Based on Nancy Freeman Patchen, *The Journey of a Master: Swami Chinmayananda: The Man, the Path, the Teaching*; Mumbai: Chinmaya Mission, Central Chinmaya Trust, 1989, 1994, p. 89.
33. Based on story recounted on *http://www.afghan-network.net/Funny/2.html* (Ret. Nov. 2015).
34. W. H. McLeod, *The B40 Janam-Sakhi*, Amritsar: Guru Nanak Dev University, 1980, p. 84.
35. Shanti Sethi, *Treasure Beyond Measure*, 2nd ed.; Beas, Punjab: RSSB, 1991, p. 244.
36. Bible, *Genesis*, 3:19.

37. Based on Osho, *Take It Easy: Talks on Zen Buddhism*, vol. 1; Pune, India: Osho International Foundation, 1981, p. 108.

38. *Idappaccayata: The Buddhist Law of Nature*, Buddhadasa Bhikkhu, translated from the Thai by Dhammaviddu Bhikkhu, Commonly Misunderstood Buddhist Principles Series No. 1; Bangkok: Bhuddadasa Foundation, Buddhadasa Indapanno Archives, 1982; Electronic edition, 2015, pp. 18–19.

39. Maharaj Sawan Singh, *Philosophy of the Masters*, vol. 1; Beas, Punjab: RSSB, 2002, p. 12.

40. Based on Swami Muktananda, *http://www.themindfulword.org/2015/life-lessons-student-ready-teacher-appears/* (Ret. Nov. 2015).

41. Plato, *The Symposium*, Speech of Aristophanes.

42. "*Dhanvante sabahee dukhee, nirdhan hain dukh roop*"; in T. R. Shangari, *Sahjobai Aur Dayabai* (Hindi), Beas, Punjab: RSSB, 2013, doha 394, p. 187.

43. C. Rajagopalachari, *Sri Ramakrishna Upanishad*; Mylapore, Madras: Sri Ramakrishna Math, 1959, ch. XXII, p. 64.

44. *Kabir Sakhi Sangrah*, 44:10; in Daryai Lal Kapur, *Call of the Great Master*; Beas, Punjab: RSSB, p. 198.

45. Tibetan saying.

46. Bernadette Roberts, in Andy Zubko, ed., *Treasury of Spiritual Wisdom*; San Diego: Blue Dove Press, 1998, p. 154.

47. Based on story in *Tales of the Mystic East*; Beas, Punjab: Science of the Soul Research Centre, pp. 70–71.

48. Based on traditional folktale.

49. Bible, *Galatians*, 6:7.

50. J. P. Vaswani, *What You Would Like to Know about Karma*; Sadhu Vaswani Center, Closter, NJ: New You Books, 2005, p. 52.

51. Annamalai Swami, in Andy Zubko, ed., *Treasury of Spiritual Wisdom*; San Diego: Blue Dove Press, 1998, p. 97.

52. Rigdzin Jigme Lingpa, Longchen Yeshe Dorje, and Kangyur Rinpoche, *Treasury of Precious Qualities: Book One*; Boston: Padmakara Translation Group, Shambhala Publications, 2011, p. 133.

53. *The Complete Works of Swami Vivekananda*, vol. 4, Calcutta: Advaita Ashrama, 2002, p. 393.

54. Mikhail Naimy, *Book of Mirdad*; London: Watkins Publishing, 2002, p. 57.

55. Thomas Merton, *New Seeds of Contemplation*; New York: New Directions Books, 1972, p. 104.

56. *Mahatma Gandhi Quotes*; *http://www.quotes.net/quote/49562* (Ret. Nov. 2015).

57. Based on traditional Native American story as told in *http://www.virtuesforlife.com/two-wolves/* (Ret. Nov. 2015).

58. Osho, *Life's Mysteries: An Introduction to the Teachings of Osho*; New Delhi: Penguin Books, 1995, p. 154.

59. Babylonian Talmud, *Tractate Pesahim*, p. 66b.

60. Attributed to Robert Green Ingersoll (1833–1899), American lawyer, agnostic, and orator. Original source not available.

61. Based on a Zen story retold in Osho in *And the Flowers Showered: The Freudian Couch and Zen*, New Delhi: Diamond Pocket Books, 2007, p. 37.

62. Tertullian, in Andy Zubko, ed., *Treasury of Spiritual Wisdom*; San Diego: Blue Dove Press, 1998, p. 321.

63. Based on Swami Chetananda, *Ramakrishna As We Saw Him*; St. Louis, Missouri: Vedanta Society of St. Louis, 1990, 2012, p. 413.

64. William Winter, *The Queen's Domain*; in Andy Zubko, ed., *Treasury of Spiritual Wisdom*; San Diego: Blue Dove Press, 1998, p. 18.

65. *Sayings of Sri Ramakrishna Paramahansa*, #78; *http://www.bhagavadgitausa.com/SayingsofSriRamakrishnaBookOne.htm* (Ret. Nov. 2015).

66. Based on *Sayings of Ramakrishna*, #318; *http://www.sacred-texts.com/hin/rls/rls28.htm* (Ret. Nov. 2015).

67. Bible, *Genesis*, 3:19.

68. Story retold from Osho, *Towards the Unknown*; New Delhi: Diamond Pocket Books, 2005, p. 114.

69. Swami Abhedananda, ed., *Sayings of Sri Ramakrishna*; New York: Cosimo Publishing Co., 2010, p. 131.

70. Swami Paramananda, in Andy Zubko, ed., *Treasury of Spiritual Wisdom*; San Diego: Blue Dove Press, 1998, p. 188.

71. *Complete Works of Swami Vivekananda*, vol. 1; Calcutta: Advaita Ashrama, 2005, p. 521.

72. Based on Osho, *Hari Om Tat Sat: The Divine Sound – That Is the Truth*; Cologne: Rebel Publishing House, 1989, p. 64.

73. Swami Abhedananda, ed., *Sayings of Sri Ramakrishna*, New York: Cosimo Classics, 2010, #252, p. 95.

74. Maharaj Sawan Singh, *Spiritual Gems*, 10th ed.; Beas, Punjab: RSSB, 2004, p. 64.

75. R. A. Nicholson, tr., *Selected Poems of Rumi*; Mineola, NY: Dover Thrift editions, 2011, p. 19; also *Treasury of Spiritual Wisdom*, p. 86.

76. Bible, *Matthew*, 6:22.

77. As retold by Pejman Aghasi in *Love: The Most Precious Gift of Life*; Lincoln, Nebraska: iUniverse, 2007, p. 79.

78. Sri Nisargadatta Maharaj, in Andy Zubko, ed., *Treasury of Spiritual Wisdom*; San Diego: Blue Dove Press, 1998, p. 460.

79. Swami Chinmayananda, *The Art of Man Making*, part 1, *Mumbai: Central Chinmaya Mission Trust*, 2008, p. 259.

80. Based on Swami Chetananda, *Ramakrishna As We Saw Him*; St. Louis, Missouri: Vedanta Society of St. Louis, 1990, 2012, p. 84.

81. Annie Besant, *The Masters*; *http://www.anandgholap.net/Masters-AB.htm* (Ret. Nov. 2015).

82. Based on Zen story retold in Angelus Silesius & Frederick Franck, *Messenger of the Heart: The Book of Angelus Silesius with Observations by the Ancient Zen Masters*; Bloomington, Indiana: World Wisdom, Inc., 2005, p. 27.

83. Bible, *Matthew*, 6:22.

84. Bhagavad Gita, ch. 11; see *http://asitis.com/11/*.

85. Guru Arjan Dev, Adi Granth, p. 394.

86. Bible, *Matthew*, 6:10.

87. St. Francis de Sales, *Introduction to the Devout Life*, 2nd revised ed., tr. & ed. Antony Mookenthattam, Bangalore: SFS. Publications, 1995, ch. 13.

88. Ibn Hasim, in Andy Zubko, ed., *Treasury of Spiritual Wisdom*; San Diego: Blue Dove Press, 1998, p. 306.

89. Based on a Taoist story retold in Osho, *Secret of Secrets: Talks on the Secret of the Golden Flower*; Antelope, Oregon: Rajneesh Foundation International, 1982, p. 750.

90. Based on Idris Shah, ed., *The Subtleties of the Inimitable Mulla Nasruddin*; London: Octagon Press, 1983, p. 102.

91. Bhai Sahib, in Andy Zubko, ed., *Treasury of Spiritual Wisdom*; San Diego: Blue Dove Press, 1998, p. 461.

92. Based on Buddhist story retold in Osho, *The Miracle: Talks on Zen*; Cologne: Rebel Publishing House, 1989, pp. 99–100.

93. Farid al-Din 'Attar, *Tadhkirat al-Awliya*, ed. Nicholson; London: 1905, I:73; in Margaret Smith, *Rabia Basri: The Mystic and Her Fellow Saints in Islam*; New Delhi: Kitab Bhavan, 2000, p. 30.

94. Maharaj Sawan Singh, *Philosophy of the Masters*, vol. II, 2nd ed.; Beas, Punjab: RSSB, 2009, p. 105.

95. Author's recollection.

96. Adapted from Swami Abhebananda, ed., *Sayings of Sri Ramakrishna*; New York: Cosimo Classics, 2010, #239, p. 91.

97. Author's recollection.

BOOKS ON SPIRITUALITY

RSSB TRADITION

Sar Bachan Prose – *Soami Ji Maharaj*
Sar Bachan Poetry – *Soami Ji Maharaj*

Spiritual Letters – *Baba Jaimal Singh*

The Dawn of Light – *Maharaj Sawan Singh*
Discourses on Sant Mat, Volume I – *Maharaj Sawan Singh*
My Submission – *Maharaj Sawan Singh*
Philosophy of the Masters (5 volumes) – *Maharaj Sawan Singh*
Spiritual Gems – *Maharaj Sawan Singh*

Discourses on Sant Mat, Volume II – *Maharaj Jagat Singh*
The Science of the Soul – *Maharaj Jagat Singh*

Die to Live – *Maharaj Charan Singh*
Divine Light – *Maharaj Charan Singh*
Light on Saint John – *Maharaj Charan Singh*
Light on Saint Matthew – *Maharaj Charan Singh*
Light on Sant Mat – *Maharaj Charan Singh*
The Path – *Maharaj Charan Singh*
Quest for Light – *Maharaj Charan Singh*
Spiritual Discourses (2 volumes) – *Maharaj Charan Singh*
Spiritual Heritage – *Maharaj Charan Singh*
Spiritual Perspectives (3 volumes) – *Maharaj Charan Singh*

Call of the Great Master – *Daryai Lal Kapur*
Concepts & Illusions: A Perspective – *Sabina Oberoi*
Heaven on Earth – *Daryai Lal Kapur*
Honest Living – *M. F. Singh*
In Search of the Way – *Flora E. Wood*
The Inner Voice – *C. W. Sanders*
Liberation of the Soul – *J. Stanley White*
Life Is Fair: The Law of Cause and Effect – *Brian Hines*
Living Meditation – *Hector Esponda Dubin*
Message Divine – *Shanti Sethi*
The Mystic Philosophy of Sant Mat – *Peter Fripp*
Mysticism: The Spiritual Path – *Lekh Raj Puri*
The Path of the Masters – *Julian P. Johnson*
Radha Soami Teachings – *Lekh Raj Puri*
A Soul's Safari – *Netta Pfeifer*
A Spiritual Primer – *Hector Esponda Dubin*
Treasure beyond Measure – *Shanti Sethi*
A Wake Up Call: Beyond Concepts & Illusions –
    Sabina Oberoi and Beverly Chapman
With a Great Master in India – *Julian P. Johnson*
With the Three Masters (3 volumes) – *Rai Sahib Munshi Ram*

MYSTIC TRADITION

Bulleh Shah – *J. R. Puri and T. R. Shangari*
Dadu: The Compassionate Mystic – *K. N. Upadhyaya*
Dariya Sahib: Saint of Bihar – *K. N. Upadhyaya*
Guru Nanak: His Mystic Teachings – *J. R. Puri*
Guru Ravidas: The Philosopher's Stone – *K. N. Upadhyaya*
Kabir: The Great Mystic – *Isaac A. Ezekiel*
Kabir: The Weaver of God's Name – *V. K. Sethi*

Many Voices, One Song: The Poet Mystics of Maharashtra – *Judith Sankaranarayan*
Mira: The Divine Lover – *V. K. Sethi*
Saint Namdev – *J. R. Puri and V. K. Sethi*
Sant Charandas – *T. R. Shangari*
Sant Paltu: His Life and Teachings – *Isaac A. Ezekiel*
Sarmad: Martyr to Love Divine – *Isaac A. Ezekiel*
Shams-e Tabrizi – *Farida Maleki*
Sheikh Farid: The Great Sufi Mystic – *T. R. Shangari*
Sultan Bahu – *J. R. Puri and K. S. Khak*
The Teachings of Goswami Tulsidas – *K. N. Upadhyaya*
Tukaram: The Ceaseless Song of Devotion – *C. Rajwade*
Tulsi Sahib: Saint of Hathras – *J. R. Puri and V. K. Sethi*
Voice of the Heart: Songs of Devotion from the Mystics

MYSTICISM IN WORLD RELIGIONS
Adventure of Faith – *Shraddha Liertz*
Buddhism: Path to Nirvana – *K. N. Upadhyaya*
The Divine Romance – *John Davidson*
The Gospel of Jesus – *John Davidson*
Gurbani Selections (Volumes I, II)
The Holy Name: Mysticism in Judaism – *Miriam Caravella*
Jap Ji – *T. R. Shangari*
The Mystic Heart of Judaism – *Miriam Caravella*
The Odes of Solomon – *John Davidson*
One Being One – *John Davidson*
Pathways to Liberation: Exploring the Vedic Tradition – *K. Sankaranarayanan*
The Prodigal Soul – *John Davidson*
The Song of Songs – *John Davidson*
Tales of the Mystic East
A Treasury of Mystic Terms, Parts I–II (10 volumes) – *John Davidson, ed.*
Yoga and the Bible – *Joseph Leeming*

VEGETARIAN COOKBOOKS
Baking Without Eggs
British Taste
Creative Vegetarian Cooking
The Green Way to Healthy Living
Meals with Vegetables

BOOKS FOR CHILDREN
The Journey of the Soul – *Victoria Jones*
One Light Many Lamps – *Victoria Jones*

MISCELLANEOUS THEMES
Empower Women: An Awakening – *Leena Chawla*
Equilibrium of Love: Dera Baba Jaimal Singh

For Internet orders, please visit: www.rssb.org

For book orders within India, please write to:
Radha Soami Satsang Beas
BAV Distribution Centre, 5 Guru Ravi Dass Marg
Pusa Road, New Delhi 110 005

ADDRESSES FOR INFORMATION AND BOOKS

INDIAN SUBCONTINENT

INDIA
The Secretary
Radha Soami Satsang Beas
Dera Baba Jaimal Singh
District Amritsar
Punjab 143 204

NEPAL
Mr. S.B.B. Chhetri
RSSB - Kathmandu
Gongabu 7, P.O. Box 1646
Kathmandu
☎ +977-01-435-7765

SRI LANKA
Mrs. Maya Mahbubani
RSSB - Colombo
No. 47/1 Silva Lane
Rajagiriya, Colombo
☎ +94-11-286-1491

SOUTHEAST ASIA

Mrs. Cami Moss
RSSB - Hong Kong
T.S.T., P.O. Box 90745
Kowloon, Hong Kong
☎ +852-2369-0625

Mr. Manoj Sabnani
RSSB - Hong Kong
27th Floor, Tower B
Billion Centre
1 Wang Kwong Road
Kowloon Bay, Hong Kong
☎ +852-2369-0625

Mrs. Ivy Sabnani
Unit D, 22nd Floor, Tower A
Billion Center
1 Wang Kwong Road
Kowloon Bay, Hong Kong

HONG KONG
RSSB - Hong Kong
27th Floor, Tower B
Billion Centre
1 Wang Kwong Road
Kowloon Bay
☎ +852-2369-0625

GUAM
Mrs. Rekha Sadhwani
625 Alupang Cove
241 Condo Lane
Tamuning 96911

INDONESIA
Mr. Ramesh Sadarangani
Yayasan RSSB - Jakarta
Jl. Transyogi Kelurahan Jatirangga
Pondok Gede 17434
☎ +62-21-845-1612

Yayasan RSSB - Bali
Jalan Bung Tomo
Desa Pemecutan Raya
Denpasar, Bali 80118
☎ +62-361-438-522

JAPAN
Mr. Jani G. Mohinani
RSSB - Kobe
1-2-18 Nakajima-Dori
Aotani, Chuo-Ku
Kobe 651-0052
☎ +81-78-222-5353

KOREA
Mr. Haresh Buxani
SOS Study Centre - Korea
638, Hopyeong-Dong
R603-1 & 604 Sungbo Building
Nam Yangju, Gyeong Gi-Do
☎ +82-231-511-7008

MALAYSIA
Mr. Bhupinder Singh
RSSB - Kuala Lumpur
29 Jalan Cerapu Satu
Off Batu 3 ¼, Jalan Cheras
Kuala Lumpur 56100
Wilayah Persekutuan
☎ +603-9200-3073

PHILIPPINES
Mr. Anil Buxani
SOS Study Centre - Manila
9001 Don Jesus Boulevard
Alabang Hills, Cupang
Muntinlupa City, 1771
Metro Manila
☎ +63-2-772-0111 / 0555

SINGAPORE
Mrs. Asha Melwani
RSSB - Singapore
19 Amber Road
Singapore 439868
☎ +65-6447-4956

TAIWAN, R.O.C.
Mr. Haresh Buxani
SOS Study Centre - Taiwan
Aetna Tower Office
15F., No. 27-9, Sec.2
Jhongjheng E.Rd.
Danshuei Township
Taipei 25170
☎ +886-2-8809-5223

THAILAND
Mr. Harmahinder Singh Sethi
RSSB - Bangkok
58/32 Thaphra Ratchadaphisek Rd.
Soi 16, Wat Thapra
Bangkok Yai District
Bangkok 10600
☎ +66-2-868-2186 / 2187

ASIA PACIFIC

AUSTRALIA
Mrs. Jill Wiley
P.O. Box 1256
Kenmore 4069
Queensland

SOS Study Centre - Sydney
1530 Elizabeth Drive
Cecil Park
New South Wales 2178
☎ +61-2-9826-2599

NEW ZEALAND
Mr. Tony Waddicor
P.O. Box 5331, Auckland

SOS Study Centre - Auckland
80 Olsen Avenue
Hillsborough, Auckland
☎ +64-9-624-2202

CANADA & UNITED STATES

CANADA
Mr. John Pope
5285 Coombe Lane, Belcarra
British Columbia V3H 4N6

SOS Study Centre - Vancouver
2932 -176th Street
Surrey, B.C. V3S 9V4
☎ +1-604-541-4792

Mrs. Meena Khanna
149 Elton Park Road
Oakville, Ontario L6J 4C2

SOS Study Centre - Toronto
6566 Sixth Line, RR 1 Hornby
Ontario L0P 1E0
☎ +1-905-875-4579

UNITED STATES
Dr. Frank E. Vogel
275 Cutts Road
Newport, NH 03773

Dr. Douglas Graham Torr
529 Carolina Meadows Villa
Chapel Hill, NC 27517

Mr. Michael Sanderson
1104 Toppe Ridge Court
Raleigh, NC 27615

Mr. Gaurav Chawla
36689 Rolf St.
Westland, MI 48186

Mr. Hank Muller
P.O. Box 1847
Tomball, TX 77377

Mr. James Rosen
6710 Round Oak Road
Penngrove, CA 94951

Dr. Vincent P. Savarese
2550 Pequeno Circle
Palm Springs, CA 92264-9522

SOS Study Centre - Fayetteville
4115 Gillespie Street
Fayetteville, NC 28306-9053
☎ +1-910-426-5306

SOS Study Centre - Petaluma
2415 Washington Street
Petaluma, CA 94954
☎ +1-707-762-5082

MEXICO & CENTRAL AMERICA

Dr. Servando Sanchez
16103 Vanderbilt Drive
Odessa, Florida 33556, USA

MEXICO
Mr. Francisco Rodriguez Rosas
RSSB - Puerto Vallarta
Circuito Universidad #779
Col. Ejido Las Juntas, Delegacion
El pitillal CP 48290
Puerto Vallarta, Jalisco
☎ +52-322-299-1954

Radha Soami Satsang Beas -
Guadalajara
Efrain Gonzalez Luna
2051 Col. Americana
Guadalajara, Jalisco 44090
☎ +52-333-615-4942

BELIZE
Mrs. Milan Bhindu Hotchandani
4633 Seashore Drive
P.O. Box 830, Belize City

PANAMA
Mr. Ashok Tikamdas Dinani
P.O. Box 0302-01000, Colon

SOUTH AMERICA

ARGENTINA
Ms. Fabiana Shilton
Leiva 4363 Capital Federal
C.P. 1427 Buenos Aires

BRAZIL
Ms. Angela Beatriz
Rua Padre Caravalito 391
Sao Paulo 05427100

CHILE
Mr. Vijay Harjani
Pasaje Cuatro No. 3438
Sector Chipana, Iquique

Fundacion RSSB - Santiago
Av. Apoquindo 4775, Oficina 1503
Las Condes, Santiago
☎ +56-22-884-6816

COLOMBIA
Mrs. Emma Orozco
Asociacion Cultural
RSSB - Medellin
Calle 48 No. 78A-30
P.O. Box 0108, Medellin
☎ +574-234-5130

ECUADOR
Mr. Miguel Egas H.
RSSB - Quito
Calle Marquez de Varela
OE 3-68y Avda. America
P.O. Box 17-21-115, Quito
☎ +5932-2-555-988

PERU
Mr. Carlos Fitts
Asociacion Cultural
RSSB - Lima
Av. Pardo #231, 12th Floor
Miraflores, Lima 18
☎ +511-651-2030

VENEZUELA
Mrs. Helen Paquin
RSSB - Caracas
Av. Los Samanes con
Av. Los Naranjos Conj
Res. Florida 335
La Florida, Caracas 1012
☎ +58-212-731-2208

CARIBBEAN

Mr. Sean Finnigan
SOS Study Centre - St. Maarten
P.O. Box 978, Phillipsburg
St. Maarten, Dutch Caribbean

Mrs. Jaya Sabnani
1 Sunset Drive South
Fort George Heights
St. Michael BB111 02
Barbados, W.I.

BARBADOS, W.I.
Mr. Deepak Nebhani
SOS Study Centre - Barbados
No. 10, 5th Avenue, Belleville
St. Michael BB11114
☎ +1-246-427-4761

CURACAO
Mrs. Hema Chandiramani
SOS Study Centre - Curacao
Kaya Seru di Milon 6-9
Santa Catharina
☎ +599-9-747-0226

ST. MAARTEN
Mr. Prakash Vishindas Daryanani
SOS Study Centre - St. Maarten
203 Oyster Pond Road
St. Maarten, Dutch Caribbean
☎ +1-721-547-0066

GRENADA, W.I.
Mr. Ajay Mahbubani
P.O. Box 820, St. Georges

GUYANA
Mrs. Indu Lalwani
155, Garnette Street
Newtown Kitty, Georgetown

HAITI, W.I
Ms. Evelyn Liautaud Quine
SOS Study Centre-Haiti
84, Autoroute de Delmas
(angle Delmas 18-A)
Saint-Martin
HT6120, Port-au-Prince

JAMAICA, W.I.
Mrs. Shamni Khiani
37A Leader Drive
Montego Bay

ST. THOMAS
Mr. Rajesh Chatlani
5178 Dronningens Gade, Ste2
US Virgin Islands
VI 00801-6145

SURINAME
Mr. Ettire Stanley Rensch
Surinamestraat 36 Paramaribo

TRINIDAD, W.I.
Mr. Chandru Chatlani
20 Admiral Court
Westmoorings-by-Sea

EUROPE

BELGIUM
Mr. Piet J. E. Vosters
Driezenstraat 26
Turnhout 2300

BULGARIA
Mr. Deyan Stoyanov
Foundation RSSB - Bulgaria
P.O. Box 39, 8000 Bourgas

CYPRUS
Mr. Heraclis Achilleos
P.O. Box 29077
1035 Nicosia

CZECH REPUBLIC
Mr. Vladimir Skalsky
Maratkova 916
142 00 Praha 411

DENMARK
Mr. Tony Sharma
Sven Dalsgaardsvej 33
DK-7430 Ikast

SOS Study Centre - Denmark
Formervangen 36
Glostrup 2600

FINLAND
Ms. Anneli Wingfield
P.O. Box 1422
00101 Helsinki

FRANCE
Mr. Pierre de Proyart
7 Quai Voltaire
Paris 75007

Mr. Bernard Estournet
1 rue de l'Arrivée
Enghien-les-Bains 95880

GERMANY and AUSTRIA
Mr. Rudolf Walberg
P.O. Box 1544
D-65800 Bad Soden

Mr. Stephan Zipplies
Auf der Platt 20
61479 Glashuetten im Ts

SOS Study Centre - Frankfurt
In den Ensterwiesen 4+9
D-61276, Weilrod-Riedelbach
Germany
☎ +49-6083-959-4700

GIBRALTAR
Mr. Sunder Mahtani
RSSB Charitable Trust - Gibraltar
15 Rosia Road, GX11 1AA
☎ +350-200-412-67

GREECE
Mr. Themistoclis Gianopoulos
6 Platonos Str.
17672 Kallithea, Attiki

SOS Study Centre - Athens
10 Filikis Etaireias Street
14234-Nea Ionia, Attiki
☎ +30-210-7010610

ITALY
Mrs. Wilma Salvatori Torri
Via Bacchiglione 3
00199 Rome

Mr. Bill Kahn
Strada Statale 63, No. 189
42044 Santa Vittoria di
Gualtieri (RE)

NETHERLANDS
Mr. Henk Keuning
Kleizuwe2
3633 AE Vreeland

Science of the Soul Study Centre -
Netherlands
Middenweg 145 E
1394 AH Nederhorst den Berg
☎ +31-294-255-255

NORWAY
Mr. Manoj Kaushal
Langretta 8
N - 1279 Oslo

POLAND
Mr. Vinod Kumar Sharma
P.O. Box 59
Ul. Szkolna 15
05-090 Raszyn

PORTUGAL
Mrs. Sharda Lodhia
CRCA Portugal
Av. Coronel Eduardo Galhardo
No.18 A-B, Lisbon 1170-105

ROMANIA
Mrs. Carmen Cismas
C.P. 6-12, 810600 Braila

SLOVENIA
Mr. Marko Bedina
Brezje pri Trzicu 68
4290 Trzic

SPAIN
Mr. J. W. Balani
Fundacion Cultural RSSB - Malaga
Avenida de las Americas s/n
Cruce Penon de Zapata
29130 Alhaurin de la Torre, Malaga
☎ +34-952-414-679

SWEDEN
Mr. Lennart Zachen
Norra Sonnarpsvägen 29
SE-286 72 Asljunga

SWITZERLAND
Mr. Sebastian Züst
Weissenrainstrasse 48
CH 8707 Uetikon Am See

UNITED KINGDOM
Mr. Narinder Singh Johal
SOS Study Centre - Haynes Park
Haynes Park, Church End Haynes
MK45 3BL Bedford
☎ +44-1234-381-234

Mr. Douglas Cameron
SOS Study Centre - Haynes Park
Haynes Park, Church End Haynes
MK45 3BL Bedford

AFRICA

BENIN
Mr. Jaikumar T. Vaswani
01 Boite Postale 951
Recette Principale, Cotonou 01

BOTSWANA
Dr. Krishan Lal Bhateja
P.O. Box 402539, Gaborone

CONGO-KINSHASA
Mr. Prahlad Parbhu
143 Kasai Ave., Lubumbashi

GHANA
Mr. Amrit Pal Singh
RSSB - Accra
P.O. Box 3976, Accra
☎ +233-242-057-309

IVORY COAST
Mr. Veerender Kumar Sapra
Avenue 7, Rue 19, Lot 196
Trechville
05 BP 1547 Abidjan 05

KENYA
Mr. Amarjit Singh Virdi
RSSB - Nairobi
P.O. Box 15134
Langata 00509, Nairobi
☎ +254-20-210-2970

LESOTHO
Mr. Tumelo Moseme
No.1 PTC Kofi Ammam Road
Maseru 0100

MADAGASCAR
Mrs. I. Rakotomahandry
BP100 Airport d'Ivato
Antananarivo 105

MAURITIUS
Mr. Indurlall Fagoonee
SOS - Mauritius
69 CNR Antelme/Stanley Avenues
Quatre Bornes
☎ +230-454-3300

MOZAMBIQUE
Mr. Mangaram Matwani
Av Josina Machel
1st floor No. 376
Maputo 190

NAMIBIA
Mrs. Jennifer Carvill
P.O. Box 449
Swakopmund 9000

NIGERIA
Mr. Nanik N. Balani
G.P.O. Box 5054, Marina Lagos

RÉUNION
Ms. Marie-Lynn Marcel
5 Chemin 'Gonneau, Bernica
St Gillesles Hauts 97435

SIERRA LEONE
Mr. Kishore S. Mahboobani
82/88 Kissy Dock Yard
P.O. Box 369, Freetown

SOUTH AFRICA
Mr. Gordon Clive Wilson
P.O. Box 1959
Randpark Ridge
Gauteng 2156

SOS Study Centre - Bush Hill
24 Kelly Road
Randburg, Bush Hill
Johannesburg 2092
☎ +27-11-025-7655

SWAZILAND
Mr. Mike Cox
Green Valley Farm
Malkerns

TANZANIA
Mr. Devender Singh Nagi
P.O. Box 1963
Dar es Salaam

UGANDA
Mr. Sylvester Kakooza
RSSB - Kampala
P.O. Box 31381, Kampala

ZAMBIA
Mr. Surinder Kumar Sachar
2922 Mutondo Crescent
Copper Belt, Kitwe 212

ZIMBABWE
Mr. Gordon Clive Wilson
P.O. Box 1959
Randpark Ridge
Gauteng 2156, South Africa

MIDDLE EAST

BAHRAIN
Mr. Sameer Deshpande
P.O. Box 75160
Juffair, Manama

ISRAEL
Mr. Michael Yaniv
Moshav Sde Nitzan 59
D.N. Hanegev 85470

KUWAIT
Mr. Jayakara Shetty
P.O. Box 22223
13083 Safat

U.A.E.
Mr. Daleep Dhalumal Jatwani
P.O. Box 37816, Dubai
☎ +971-4-339-4773